Kirsty's Story

Kirsty Ashton

authorHOUSE

AuthorHouse™ UK Ltd.
500 Avebury Boulevard
Central Milton Keynes, MK9 2BE
www.authorhouse.co.uk
Phone: 08001974150

© 2011. Kirsty Ashton. All rights reserved
No part of this book may be reproduced, stored in a retrieval system, or transmitted by any means without the written permission of the author.

First published by AuthorHouse   1/5/2011

ISBN: 978-1-4567-7047-1(sc)
ISBN: 978-1-4567-7048-8(hc)

Any people depicted in stock imagery provided by Thinkstock are models, and such images are being used for illustrative purposes only.
Certain stock imagery © Thinkstock.
This book is printed on acid-free paper.
Because of the dynamic nature of the Internet, any Web addresses or links contained in this book may have changed since publication and may no longer be valid. The views expressed in this work are solely those of the author and do not necessarily reflect the views of the publisher, and the publisher hereby disclaims any responsibility for them.

Please observe the following rules before reading this book

Please do not feel sorry for me –

I'm cool about it.

Please don't think to yourself "poor girl" –

I'm very happy.

Do not shed a tear whilst reading this book –

You will only get the pages wet and won't be able to read the book and we would not want that.

Please do sit back and enjoy this book –

And you'll make me very happy.

With love from

Kirsty x x x

www.kirstysstory.co.uk

Living with Neurofibromatosis

Contents

Introduction	1
About me	3
Living with Neurofibromatosis (NF1) and Scoliosis	8
Scoliosis Surgery	25
Since being discharged from hospital	56
How mum and dad coped	130
What is Neurofibromatosis?	136
Neurofibromatosis Question and Answers	144
What is Scoliosis?	148
What is a Boston Brace?	151
The facts about my condition from my doctors	156
What other people have to say	163
Some fun times	173
My Goal - Fund raising	222
Some of the Celebrities that I have met	224
Supporters	240
My Goals in life	244
Charities	246
Glossary	249
Acknowledgements	255

Introduction

In 1998 Kirsty was enjoying weekly swimming lessons; and she had also joined the same dance school as her brother (Christopher). Chris had been having dance lessons for a few years and Kirsty wanted to dance on a stage like her brother and was looking forward to her next stage show. Ten years on and Kirsty can no longer dance or swim as well as she could when she was eight years old. She had to give it all up due to being in so much pain.

She depends on elbow crutches and use's a power scooter when out shopping and needs help with some of her everyday needs.

Kirsty's story tells how and why her life changed due to the problems caused by Neurofibromatosis and Scoliosis.

When Kirtsy was 11 weeks old she was diagnosed with Neurofibromatosis (NF1), which caused no problems until she was eight years old when she was also diagnosed with scoliosis. She now lives a very different, but full life, where she is surrounded by her family and a large group of friends, some of whom have made a contribution to this book with their own thoughts.

Kirsty Ashton

What happened to change Kirsty's life so much?

An operation at The Manchester's Children's Hospital in March 2005 to place two titanium rods on ether side of Kirsty's spine came with risk. Eight hours into the twelve hour operation the surgeon had to stop due to complications. Kirsty was wheeled to HDU where she remained very poorly for the next four days. The surgeon needed to ask for further advice on what to do next and said he had never before seen so many tumours on anyone's spine.

A second eight hour operation was planned a few days later but Kirsty had taken a turn for the worse and was too poorly to have such a big operation, which was put on hold twice.

Eventually the operation went ahead, but Kirsty continued to be very poorly and was hospitalised for three months. She spent her birthday in hospital and since leaving hospital in June 2005 she has undergone many more operations and still attends hospital a least once a week.

Kirsty's story is a remarkable one. Physically she remains weakened by her condition but her personality and character remains undamaged. Supported by her family and friends, Kirsty is as busy as ever she was. Whether she is studying, fundraising or writing her blog and helping others with NF and Scoliosis, she is a role model for all young people, having won many awards, for which she has been nominated by her teachers, family and members of the public.

About me

I was born on the 5th April 1990 in Wythenshawe Hospital, Wythenshawe, Manchester, weighing in at 6lb 13oz. My big brother, Christopher picked my name (Kirsty). I have a nick name which all my close friends call me, which is Kay, and my other nick name is "Titch" as I am the smallest one of all my friends.

I'm told I was a happy baby and always blowing bubbles with my mouth. Soon after I was born, mum noticed some brown marks on my skin (cafe-au-lait" spots) and mentioned them to the pediatric doctor when he did his ward round, the doctor dismissed the marks saying it was nothing to worry about. But my mum knew different and at 11 weeks old I was diagnosed with Neurofibromatosis (NF1). My mum also has this condition so it came as no surprise to her.

When I was about 8 month old I was modeling for Tuesday's Child and did some catalogue work. Mum said everyone loved me because I could whistle by the age of 11 month and I was also out of nappies by the time I was a year old and every time the cameraman went to take a picture I would hold myself and shout "POT", which meant I needed the potty.

Kirsty Ashton

I started walking just before my 1st birthday and pretty much on target with all the health checks that babies have. The only thing I had to do was visit the hospital every six months to keep an eye on my NF for any problems that could crop up.

I was fine up until the age of eight, I enjoyed swimming, dance and gym classes, I had even managed to complete my Gold badge and mile swim before I was 9 years old, which I was really pleased about.

My favourite colour is blue and I'm not really a girlie girl, I don't like dresses but love my jeans and tops.

I don't let my disabilities get me down. I enjoy raising money for other poorly children, who have different illness not just Neurofibromatosis, I work very closely with the charity When You Wish Upon A Star, I raise X amount of money for a trip and pass it over to the wish team so they are able to put the wish of another poorly child into action.

I joined Peel Hall Primary school in the September of 1995 where I stayed until I moved on to Altrincham College of Arts in the September of 2001. Although I missed almost a year of schooling in year 10, I still managed to pass 15 G.C.S.E's / G.N.V.Q's, nine of them being A-C grade. My English teacher said I was mild Dyslexic and helped me all he could. When I came out of hospital I had lessons at home three hours a week.

I attended college doing a National Diploma in Performing Arts which was a 2 year course. In 2006, two of my overall grades were Merits

I live at home with my mum, dad and big brother Chris, and have always lived in the same house.

My mum, Julie

My mum and I are very close. She has always been there for me and tends not to let thing bother her, unless Chris or I are ill that is. We have the same sense of humour and we have been known to borrow each other's clothes.

Mum stayed with me all the time I was in hospital and even slept on a chair next to my bed for two months. I often kid people and say my mum is my big sister: well, she is young looking for her age. I also love going to bingo with my mum, gone are the days when bingo was for the older generation.

My mum also suffers from Neurofibromatosis NF1, mum was not diagnosed until the age of 10 years. My mum found a small lump on the side of her tummy and told her mum about it after visiting the doctors my mum was sent to the hospital for more test at which time she was diagnosed with NF.

Kirsty Ashton

My dad, John

My dad and I are very different and don't always see eye to eye. But he's always there for me, I love him and he is a great dad.

My dad was unable to stay in hospital due to work commitments but came to see me almost every day.

My dad works hard to provide for our family so is not able to attend my hospital visits with me, but he always asks how I have got on and wants to know what the doctors have said.

Kirsty's Story

My brother, Christopher

Chris is three and half years older than I. We only argue over silly things really, like whose had the last can of coke and who is better looking, which we both know is me, or something really silly and unimportant. He's always looked out for me and is a protective big brother.

My brother would turn up at the hospital after work sometimes this would be as late as 10pm, the nurses ect, would still let him in as they knew how much it meant to me to see my brother and we never made any noise, well, we tried not to.

I hope my brother knows how much I love him. and knows I'll always be there for him.

Kirsty's story

Living with Neurofibromatosis (NF1) and Scoliosis

Summer of 1998:
I use to attend weekly swimming lessons at my local swimming baths from the age of 5 years old, which I really enjoyed. I made friends with another little girl of the same age, Jess. We both would compete against each other to see who could pass the next swimming badge first and our mums would give each of us £1.00 when we did well.

I was doing really well with my swimming lessons and even managed to pass my Gold badge and 1 mile swim when I was 8 years old (so did Jess). I remember one day the instructor asked to speak to my mum and mentioned that I had suddenly started to kick my leg out to the side and that I had slowed down a lot. The instructor asked if I had been having any problems with my back, to which mum said "No".

Kirsty's Story

It was only when I attended the hospital for my six month check-up a few weeks later that we found out why.

You know how you always hear those stories on TV and in the papers, etc. about people with these illnesses, conditions and pain, but you never even imagine it would happen to you. Well, for me it did. I was told I had Scoliosis. Never heard of it? Neither had I really.

October 1998:
It was October 1998 and during my annual NF check-up at my local hospital in Wythenshawe I saw a pediatrician, (a doctor who specializes in children's illnesses). He did all the normal test including my Blood pressure (I loved having my blood pressure done and asked mum and dad if I could have a real blood pressure machine of my own at home, which they bought for me, I would put the cuff round the arm of anybody who would trust me to do so and I would just pump and pump not thinking how tight the cuff was getting on the person. They would be shouting for me to stop and I would just giggle). Anyway the doctor then asked me to bend over and touch my toes. It was at this point the doctor looked concerned.

The doctor asked my mum how long I had had the curve in my spine. Mum said that she was not aware that I had any curve in my spine so he sent me off for an x-ray of my spine and said not to worry he would see me in 6 months. Four days later mum received a phone call from the hospital doctor, who had looked at the x-rays and was not happy with the results and mum was to bring me back to the hospital the next day.

I remember mum was upset by this news, I did not know what was wrong, I felt fine. I got the day off school "Yes!" When we went in to see the doctor (Mr. Kurdy) he said that the x-ray results showed a curvature in my spine, Mr. Kurdy was an Orthopaedic Surgeon (Orthopaedic surgeons specialise in disorders of the muscles and bones). Mr. Kurdy thought it best if I had an MRI scan of my spine to see what was causing the curve. We went home and waited for the appointment to come.

Kirsty Ashton

23rd December 1998:
Time for my scan, which was to be the first of many. I had to take anything off that was metallic and mum had to remover, her jewellery that took about 20 minutes, only joking, I also had to remove my jeans because of the zip, I walked in the room with my mum, which was no bigger than my bedroom, so we are talking small. I thought the scan room looked pretty cool, lots of gadgets and cool paintings on the wall, all I had to do was lie down and keep very still for 1 hour (a long time for me to keep still) so that the images they took would be absolutely clear.

I was allowed to take my own music to be played. Guess what I took? The Smurfs Christmas Hits. The doctors were laughing at it. Mum was allowed to stay with me; but they would not let one of my teddies into the scan room (Adam), due to the metal that was inside him. The doctor explained that anything metallic can make the image go blurry. So the doctor propped him up at the window to watch me. The radiographer (Ken) operated the scanner from another room, which was separated from us by a glass window. Ken kept talking to me through the headphones that I was wearing and asking if I was ok.

Lying in the scanner is bit like being in a small tunnel that is open at both ends. I had to lie on this really narrow bed, which moved into the scanner and my face was only centimetres away from the top. I had to stay completely still. The bed was then moved now and again to scan different parts of my spine.

The scan machine was really noisy. It sounded like one of those drill diggers in the street. Mum was given ear plugs and I wore headphones so that I could listen to my CD. Mum said the ear plugs did not really help.

I had been in the scanner for about 30 minutes when the doctor came into the room and said that I needed an injection of contrast dye. It was so the scan would make certain tissues and blood vessels show up more clearly and with a much greater detail on the scan.

Good job mum had put some magic cream on my arm so the injection would not hurt. Scan over and time to go home. They would not tell us the results until the doctor had looked at all the scans.

Kirsty's Story

January 1999:
I was back at the hospital for my results. The news was not good. The scan had shown that I had a number of tumours on my spine. One of the tumours was pushing my spine to one side, which was causing the scoliosis. My mum was told not to worry as it was only a small curve, but under the circumstance's I was to be transferred to Pendlebury Children's Hospital to go under the care of the doctor who specializes in scoliosis.

March 1999:
I went to Pendlebury Children's Hospital. I saw a really nice doctor called Mr. Spillsbury (he was very funny). He did loads of test on me including my reflexes and a neurological examination where he asked me to close my eyes and I had to tell him when he touched me if it felt sharp or soft. He then sent me for more x-rays of my spine; we had to wait while Mr. Spillsbury looked at the x-ray films. Mr. Spillsbury had a long chat with my parents, I can't say I understood what he was saying with all the medical words that were being used (I was only 8 years old). But my mum explained that the doctor wanted me to have an MRI scan of my spine done again before any decision was made.

May 1999:
Back at the hospital for my scan and the same routine as last time. Only this time I took my NOW 47 CD with me.

June 1999:
I went back to see Mr. Spillsbury for my scan results.

Mr. Spillsbury said that the scan had confirmed the presence of numerous tumours at the lumbar junction extending well into the sacrum. As I felt ok he considered it best that he just kept an eye on things for now to make sure things did not get any worse. I had lots of visits to hospital during the rest of the year.

December 1999:
My brother had been keeping a secret from me. He had arranged for me to go to Lapland to meet the real Santa, I had always wanted to go. My brother said I had been so brave that he wrote to "When You Wise upon a Star" and told them all about how brave I had been and to ask if they could make my wish come true and they did. I had a great day.

Kirsty Ashton

My dad came with me as my mum had only just come out of hospital after having a very big operation (a hysterectomy) and was not allowed to fly. We had to be at the airport at 5am, Chris and mum came to wave us off at the airport.

I had a ride on a quad bike, went sledging and of course I had to have a sleigh ride which was pulled by Rudolph. Lots of Celebrities accompanied us and joined in the fun with the all the children in the snow. When we met Santa lots of the grown ups got very emotional. My friends at school had written letters to Santa and asked me if I would hand them to him, which I did. It was the perfect start to my Christmas, and I made many friends. It was just magical."

Thanks go to my brother and everyone at "When You Wish upon a Star" for making this dream come true.

March 2000:
Back at Pendlebury Children's Hospital and I'm sent for an x-ray as soon as I get there. We waited for the x-ray film so I could give it to Mr. Spillsbury. I still felt fine, but this time the news was not good. The doctor was concerned that in the last four months my spine had curved a further 9 degrees. He was very keen to operate; I was only nine and did not really understand what was happening. We were due to go on holiday and I did not want to miss it (I was looking forward to going away). We could not go away last year due to all the hospital appointments I had. Mr. Spillsbury being the nice doctor he is, decided that I could still go on holiday and said he would talk more about the operation when I got back home from holiday.

Back home from hospital:
A couple of days later the phone rang, it was Mr. Spillsbury to say he had been looking at my x-rays again and that he would feel happier if I wore a Boston Brace to help support my spine while I was away and up until the operation on my spine was carried out.

So I had to go back to the hospital for a fitting of the brace, which had to be custom made for me, I was asked to strip off down to my under clothes I was then wrapped in plaster cast to make the mould for the brace and I had to stand really still until the cast dried. This only took a

Kirsty's Story

few minutes then the cast was cut away from me and sent away to be made into a back brace.

Two weeks later the brace was ready. I walked into the hospital room not knowing what to expect. The brace was really hard and went around my body and fashioned at the back with Velcro straps that had to be pulled really tight. I was told I would have to wear the brace 23 hours a day and that it would take about 8 weeks for me to build up to wearing it for so long. Even though the brace was uncomfortable I decided to keep it on while I travelled home that day.

Mum and dad said I had done really well and I think it was down to the praise that I kept getting from my parents that after only three days, I was managing to wear the brace twenty-three hours a day. Mr. Spillsbury was really pleased with me and called me his little star. My mum, dad and brother was really proud too. The brace did look a bit boring so my mum jazzed it up a bit and stuck Pekachu stickers on it for me.

I loved stickers and every time I had to have a blood test taken I would ask for a sticker (I put them on my brace too). I think liking sticker's so much comes from when mum would give my brother and me stickers to put on our chart for being good and we would both get treats at the end of each week.

Holiday time:
I was really sweaty wearing the brace. Imagine being in Spain with the temperature reaching 102 degrees and wearing a plastic jacket with an under shirt on too, believe me, I was hot. I got to take it off when I went swimming. GREAT! I was not bothered if people saw my brace: it was now part of me and when I got too hot I would take my top shirt off, "Yes", people did turn and look at me but I just smiled one of my cheeky smiles at them and they would smile back. It was the kids that would ask me why I was wearing the brace, I would be honest and tell them that I had a poorly back and no more questions were asked.

Home from Holiday:
Mr. Spillsbury asked to see me and after doing further x-rays of my spine both in and out of the brace it was decided that the brace was holding my spine in a much better position. The brace was working and

Kirsty Ashton

keeping my spine supported and surgery is now planned for when I am 13. I know I am going to be in a brace for a very long time, I don't mind if it helps. I will need a new brace every four to six months depending on how quickly I grow. I have been told I will have to wear the brace for at least two years after surgery too.

People ask me if I am in pain.
The simple answer is "Yes". Some times I get a lot of pain in my back and legs, I also get very tired. I need help with some personal care and I cannot bend down so my brother helps me with anything I cannot do. I thought I would look fat in the brace, but you cannot tell I am wearing it and it holds my belly in as I have a bit of a pot belly.

In school assembly, I'd sit on one of those chairs with holes at the top due to the pain in my back and not being able to sit on the floor. But when I went to get up, the brace got caught on the back of the chair and I'd stand up with the chair attached to me. Apart from a couple of friends, everyone else used to sit there and laugh. It was awful. At High School (Altrincham College of Arts in Altrincham) it got even worse. I wasn't able to do any sport because I couldn't run about. The only thing I could do was football and I was always the goalkeeper.

My brace was like body armour and I'd stand in the net and belly butt the ball. But some kids were evil and shouted "Cardboard Cutout" at me. It was very upsetting and I spoke to my head teacher about it. But they advised me to ignore it in the hope that they'd stop doing it. They didn't give in though. It was only when I went into hospital for the operation that they realised how serious it was. The bullies then felt bad and rang me up to find out how I was.

One of the boys who cruelly called me "cardboard cutout" at school contacted me on Facebook. He got in touch to say sorry for everything he'd done and asked if I would forgive him. It was very upsetting at the time but I replied back saying it was all in the past and that long as he'd grown up then I'd like to be his friend. Life is too short to hold grudges.

Kirsty's Story

New School:
I have just started at a new school and I was a little worried about it at first but my brother attends the same school and he has promised to look after me.

My brother puts my brace on for me and I really love my brother. He is simply the best.

My brother and I both won the Child of Achievement award this year, Chris won it for a child safety book that he wrote, which he gave out to schools and hospitals and for the way he helps me. I won it for coping so well with my condition. We had to go to London for the awards and we met loads of celebrities. When we got back we both were asked to do a TV interview for our local Granada TV News and were in the papers, I felt like a star my self.

August 2001:
Getting some pain in my groin when walking, and some new lumps have appeared, one on my foot and at the back of my ear. Mum made an appointment with our family doctor who thought I may have a viral infection. I was put on antibiotics and was asked to come back in three weeks if things were no better.

3 weeks later:
Lumps are bigger now, so the doctor sends me off to the hospital to have them looked at.

October 2001:
The Doctor is not sure what is going on, and wants a second opinion from an orthopaedic doctor.

In the mean time I am off to Spain for 7 days. When I get home I have to go and see my family doctor as things are no better.

November 2001:
Back at my local hospital the nurse tells me that I have lost weight. When I go in to see the doctor he is surprised to know that I had not seen the orthopaedic doctor so he phones him to tell him of the situation and I was given an appointment for the 7th January 2002.

Kirsty Ashton

December 2001:
I am at the Manchester Children's Hospital to see my favourite doctor Mr. Spillsbury; the nurse sends me for an x-ray of my spine before seeing Mr. Spillsbury. When I go in to see Mr. Spillsbury I mentioned that I had been getting a lot of pain in my groin, Mr. Spillsbury, did some test on me and asked me to stand on one leg, which I had difficulty in doing. He was not very happy with my hip and commented that one hip was a lot higher than the other so he wants me to have a bone scan in January 2002 and MRI scan done of my spine in February 2002. He did have some good news though. On looking at my x-rays my spine had not got any worse since my last visit, which was great news: The brace is still doing its job and stopping my spine from getting any worse.

Mr. Spillsbury is really happy with the x-rays and gets one of his doctors to come and have a look at it. My next stop is to see Mike Gilligan who is an Orthotist, a maker and fitter of Orthopaedic appliances, (Mike, makes my back braces for me) Mike is really nice; I have grown so I need a new one. Mike tells me it will be ready in January 2002. When I arrived back home I had received a package in the post it was a new teddy that my friend Bill Hicks who lives in Scotland sent me. He had won the teddy in the office raffle and decided to give it to me as he knows how much I like teddies.

7th January 2002:
I went for my bone scan today; they used a special scanner called a gamma camera. I was given a small amount of special fluid called a tracer, which will show up my bones. The tracer contains a very small amount of radiation, which the gamma camera can "See" and builds up a picture of me. I had to have a small injection to put the tracer into my blood stream; they use a special needle called a butterfly. Mum put some magic cream on the back of my hand one hour before, so the needle would not hurt. I had to lie very still on the bed; I did not feel anything when the pictures were being taken. Mum came in with me. We were able to watch Postman Pat on the TV while I was having the scan.

January 2002:
Today, I went for the scan on my spine; it was to see if the tumours had grown from the last scan that I had.

Kirsty's Story

22nd January 2002:
I went to Pendlebury children's hospital for my results. The results are good, and there were no changes to the size of the tumours on my spine. I have got to go and see Mr. Kurdy over the tumours growing in my foot. I have been getting a lot of discomfort when I am walking. Mr. Spillsbury informed me that he was leaving too, I was not very happy about this news, I had built up a lot of trust with him and now I have got to start all over again. I was upset and told him I did not want him to go. He was moving on to Birmingham Children's Hospital and said if I wanted he would still see me but it would mean me be being transferred to Birmingham Children's Hospital. Doing that would have made things even more difficult for my parents so I decided to see what my new doctor would be like.

25th February 2002:
Time to see Mr. Kurdy, who is not sure what to do about the tumours in my foot. I am being referred to a plastic Surgeon so he/she can have a look at my foot.

In the meantime I am kept busy with many other hospital visits. Having scans, X-rays and blood test have become a regular thing for me.

November 2002:
My brother has won a big award for the way in which he helps me and for the safety books he has written plus other work he does. The award is called The Young Citizen of the Year; it is awarded by the Greater Manchester Police. He was nominated by Miss Lloyd, our head teacher. We were both on Granada Reports and we went to an award ceremony in Manchester. Chris was named the young citizen of the year for Trafford by the Greater Manchester Police. I'm really proud of my brother.

1st May 2003: Result time:
I was back at Wythenshawe hospital to find out the results of a scan that I had done on my neck about 5 weeks ago.

My height and weight were checked (yes! I am taller than my mum). Then I am off to see Pam (the play leader) Pam knows me very well, I have been going to the hospital since I was 11 weeks old, Pam has watched me grow up. Anyway we have a chat and I decide to do a painting. Just as I get stuck into my painting the doctor calls me in, always the way. Pam puts my painting to one side so I can finish it when I come out from seeing the doctor.

Bad news:
The doctor had some bad news for me. Unfortunately the scan that I had done on my neck shows that I have lots of tumours in my neck, he is unsure if this is what is causing my headaches. He wants me to see a neurosurgeon for a second opinion.

4th June 2003:
Mum and Dad took me to the teddy factory in the Trafford centre today. They bought me a new teddy (a dog) to bring me luck. He is really nice and I bought one too. The one mum and dad bought me I called Scan and the one I bought I called Stella. It was really cool, I helped stuff them both then I put a little red heart in them while making a wish (I cannot tell you my wish just yet, it may not come true if I do).

July 2003:
I went for a scan on my spine at Pendlebury Children's Hospital this morning (I am getting use to all these scans now). There was a really bad accident on the motorway so we were very late for my appointment (the doctors understood and had heard about the accident). The scan took about 30 minutes this time. Mum came in with me and so did my two new teddies, Scan and Stella. I tried to listen to my Robbie Williams C.D 2 but it was difficult to hear. Scan over, the doctor came in to see me but could not tell me the results. He said they have to be sent to my consultant first. I was feeling a little dizzy and sick so the doctor asked me to sit on the end of the bed for a while until I felt better.

Holiday time: July 2003:
We are off on holiday to Florida and I will be told my results when I get back.

August 2003:
I had a really nice holiday, which you can read more about later in my book.

Kirsty's Story

Result time August 2003:
I met my new doctor Mr. Neil Oxborrow, I don't know what it was but I liked Mr. Oxborrow from the word go I felt relaxed and comfortable talking to him, even if he did have bad news for me.

Mr. Oxborrow looked at my scan and told me that the main tumour had started to grow and this is the reason I am getting so much pain. He looked at my x-ray and points out that the curve in my spine has worsened too, but only by 9 degrees.

Mr. Oxborrow was not happy by the results. He goes and mentions these latest results to another doctor (Mr. Wattson) who then came in to have a chat with me. He was concerned by the fact that the tumour had started to grow and the fact that my back had also started to worsen. The doctor asked me if I was happy with the way my back was looking and then said he would operate on my spine if I wanted him too. I was a little shocked, I told him I needed time to think, I was not expecting the decision to be mine and I am not sure if I want to be the one to make the decision, I am only thirteen, I didn't think for one minute it would be my decision.

The doctor arranged for me to have this special scan done before I went home and I have got to have it done again in 6 months. In the meantime I have got to see a neurosurgeon over the tumour, which has started to grow.

August 2003:
Back at Wythenshawe hospital to see the doctor over the tumours in my neck. I won't go in to everything that was said, but basically, I have got to see a plastic surgeon over having some of the tumours removed from my neck.

Back home:
After going shopping with my gran, the phone rings. It's the doctor-asking mum to bring me back to the hospital that afternoon. They wanted to take some photos of my neck for the plastic surgeon to see.

29th October 2003:
I had to go and see the plastic surgeon today over the tumours in my neck, foot and the one on my chin. He said that if he tried to remove the tumour from my chin it would leave a nasty scar and that it may be better left alone at the moment. Unfortunately there are too many tumours in my neck to try and remove any of them, I have about eight tumours on each side of my neck, which are not too big but you can see them when I turn my head to the side. I am going back to see the doctor after Christmas and if any of them have grown he may have to rethink and operate on them.

5th November 2003:
I went to see the neurosurgeon (Mr. Thorn) today; he was really nice and took the time to explain my scan results to me. Mr. Thorn pinned my scan pictures up to a light so that he could show them to me and pointed out where the tumours were. He pointed to some dots on the scan and explained that all the dots that I could see were tumours. Some are over 4cm in size and it is a bit scary to see so many dots on my scan and find it hard to believe they are tumours.

Mr. Thorn wants me to have a special spine scan done, which will give him a more detailed picture of my spine. He also wants to discuss my case with a Professor before any decisions are made about trying to remove any of the tumours from my spine. There are too many tumours on my spine to try and remove them all so he wants to make sure that he removes the correct ones and needs to discuss this with the Professor first.

Date for scan on my spine:
I have now got the date for my scan, I go on the 15th December 2003. I have been told I will need a needle this time so mum is going to put the magic cream on the back of my hand first so that it will not hurt.

29th December 2003:
I went to see Dr. Liberman, who is a chronic pain specialist, he tells me he normally only sees adults but because they don't have a pain clinic for children in Manchester he agreed to see me. He was really nice, we had a long chat and he gave me a good checking over.

Kirsty's Story

Dr. Liberman decided to give me a T.E.N.s Machine to take home, which I have to wear under my brace and 2 lots of cream, which I have to have rubbed into my side and onto my foot. A T.E.N.s machine is a Transcoutaneous Electrical Nerve Stimulation (T.E.N's) drug free method of controlling pain. It uses tiny electrical impulses sent through the skin to the nerves to modify my pain perception. I think I am coping very well with it, although it is a little uncomfortable under the brace.

My back feels a lot worse now:
I have been getting a lot more pain in my back and it feels a so it has gone worse, I have got to go back to Pendlebury Children's hospital on the 30th January 2004. I should find out my scan results too. Unfortunately I don't feel very well at the moment.

30th January 2004:
I have now received the results of my scan and unfortunately the spine has worsened yet again and one of the tumours has grown yet again. Doctors think it is time for my operation (I am really scared). The neurosurgeon and the orthopaedic doctors are going to have a meeting over what happens next. In the mean time I have got to use my T.E.N's machine to help with the pain. The doctor doesn't think the brace is doing me any good now, but I have worn it 23 hours a day for over five years and my back really aches when I don't have it on.

I'm very upset at the moment:
I am upset at the moment. My gran was taken into hospital on an emergency 999 call. Gran phoned us very upset saying she was hemorrhaging. When we got there my gran was in a mess, so we called for an ambulance which came within minutes. Gran was in hospital for 2 weeks and was diagnosed with lung cancer (we were all very upset by the news). Gran was only home 2 days when she was rushed back in again and again she was in hospital for 2 weeks. My gran came home feeling not very well and with a lot to think about, I had to think how I could help my gran with this dreadful news. She's my gran and I love her so much. I went to see gran everyday while she was in hospital and sometimes twice a day. My gran has just been back in hospital after having half her left lung removed (a big operation for a lady of 76 years); gran was on the H.D.U. for a week very poorly. She looks as though she may have had a stroke as her mouth looks to have drooped to one side. I kept telling her how much I loved her and wanted her to get better

and that I needed her to be there for me when I have my operation. My gran is now home, still feeling a bit poorly but she is with me and I know my gran will be there for me when I have my operation, because she loves me as much as I love her.

1st April 2004:
Just received a call from Mr. Oxborrow at Pendlebury children's hospital. He still working out how best to go about my operation and is trying to set up a meeting with other doctors to discuss the situation. He will phone again next week.

16th August 2004:
For the past few months I have just been in contact with my doctors over the phone while it was being decided what happens next.

18th August 2004:
I went to see Mr. Thorn today over the tumours on my spine and the news was not good. Mr. Thorn told me that he had been looking at the scans again and decided to get a second opinion He admitted that he does not feel confident enough to touch any of the tumours on my spine as there are far too many. He explained that some of the tumours are only small but some are on a much larger scale. He explained the risk of me coming out of surgery paralysed was high if he attempted to remove any of the tumours. He did say he would like to be present when Mr. Oxborrow puts the rods in my back for my scoliosis surgery and if at that time things look different he will try and remove some. In the mean time he wanted to talk with another surgeon about my spine to ask his opinion.

10th September 2004:
Back to Pendlebury Children's Hospital to see Mr. Oxborrow who talks to me over what Mr. Thorn had said to him and then sends me off for an x-ray. When I go back in his room Mr. Oxborrow tells me my spine has worsened yet again and that he thinks it's going to continue to worsen. I have been in a lot of pain and finding it difficult to do some things due to the pain.

Mr. Oxborrow tells me he will need to operate before Christmas and that the next time he sees me will be on my pre operation check. I'm not really frightened by the operation. Well, maybe I am just a little

Kirsty's Story

bit (at least I'll get some time off school), but on second thoughts, not really for I'm told I'll have a home tutor and my school has been really good to me.

I'm going to have my operation done down the side of my body so no one can see the scar.

13th September 2004:
I went to see Miss. Brains at Christie Hospital today over the tumours in my foot and the one growing on my chin.

Miss. Brains was really nice and she said it would be best if they removed the tumours and she gave me the date there and then (19th October 2004). I am going to be awake when they do this operation. Can't say I'm looking forward to being awake for surgery. Mum is having two tumours removed at the same time by the same surgeon so we will look after each other.

19th October 2004:
I had the operation on my foot, ankle and chin today at Christie Hospital. I had three tumours removed under a local anaesthesia. This meant that the areas surrounding the tumours were made numb (anaesthetized) so that I did not feel any pain during the surgery and I remained awake too. I was able to eat and drink as normal before surgery. My surgeon tested the area to make sure that skin was numb before starting the surgery. All I could feel was a little pressure, pulling and pushing but no sharp needle type pain. My surgeon told me to tell her if I felt any pain during surgery and she would give me some more local anaesthetic.

It takes about 6 hours for the numb feeling to go away so I had to be very careful until the normal feeling returned. I had eight stitches in my foot, four stitches in my ankle and three stitches put in my chin. I have got to have the stitches in my chin removed in seven days and the stitches in my foot and ankle in fourteen days. When I got home I had a lie down for a while then my brother took me out to buy me a get well present (2 DVD's). Told you what great brother I have.

I was in a lot of pain so my mum gave me some paracetamol. Hopefully the scars will not be so noticeable in another four to six months time. I am not in school for the rest of the week and next week I am on half term. Hopefully by then the swelling will have gone down and I will be able to put my shoes on.

Mum was feeling ok after her surgery and not in too much pain.

Time for stitches to come out:
When the nurse came to change the dressing on my foot she said the scar was infected and a clean dressing was put on my foot, I had to go back a few days later to have the stitches out. The stitches in my chin came out ok and I'm left with a small scar. Back for stitches out of foot and ankle and dressing change. Foot still looking no better so a swab was taken of the yucky stuff coming from my foot and the wound was covered with gauze and I was put on antibiotics, I had to go back every other day so the nurse could change the dressing. I'm now on my third lot of antibiotics and the scar has still not closed. The nurse tells me it's going to take a long time to heal. She was right. It was weeks and weeks before it started to heal and the scar does not look good. Good job it was my foot that looks such a mess and not my chin.

1st December 2004:
Mr. Thorn at Pendlebury Children's Hospital asked to see me today. He said he wanted to explain what was happening and what he had been doing over the past few weeks.

He told me that he had recently had many meetings with other doctors to discuss the results of my last lot of scans and that I had one large tumour on my spine and many smaller ones and that there were many abnormalities to the spine. He explained that all the doctors that he had spoken to were of the same opinion and that if they tried to remove any of the tumours it could cause paralysis (the risk of this was high). Mr. Thorn was very apologetic, saying it was his fault that the operation had been held up, but he wanted to make sure he was doing the right thing. The operation on my spine will now be done in the New Year.

Scoliosis Surgery

19th January 2005:
I attended Pendlebury children's hospital for my pre-operation assessment. This was to check that I was fit for the operation and to make sure I knew what would happen and why. I was sent for an x-ray of my spine. Many x-rays were taken in different positions, I then I had to go back to clinic and wait to see Pauline (Scoliosis Nurse Specialist). Pauline had a long chat with my parents and me and said I may need a blood transfusion after surgery and had I thought about having an Autologous blood donation, which meant I would be my own blood donor. My mum asked if she could be a blood donor for me, but they said "No" and that if my mum was to be the donor it would be no different from anyone else being the donor. So I decided that I would give my own blood.

The blood donation procedure
A blood sample was taken from my thumb (waaaaa, I have to say this made me jump and it hurt, the little Vampire). This was done to check the iron level in my blood. I had to take an iron supplement for a few weeks (three iron tablets a day) before I could donate the blood, which would be done in about three weeks later.

My blood pressure was taken and I had to do a lung function test, The Lung function tests were done to measure how well my lungs were working before surgery. I was asked to perform various breathing exercises using a number of instruments which measure different aspects of my lung function. One of the tests I did was to look at how fast I could blow air out through my airways and also how fast I could breathe air back in. This test helped the doctor measure the flow of air to and from my lungs and airways. I had to breathe in until my lungs were completely filled with air before blowing out as hard and as fast as I could through a mouthpiece into a measuring device. Doing the lung function test made me really tired and a little dizzy. All the lung function tests I did were normal.

When I went back to donate my blood I had to have another thumb prick waaaaaaa... and a nerve conduction test done.

Time for a chat with Mr. N Oxborrow (my scoliosis doctor)
Mr. Oxborrow looked at the x-rays then took a pencil and ruler and began marking measurements of the curvature on the x-ray; he was not happy with the x-ray results and kept shaking his head and saying that they must be wrong.

Mr. Oxborrow asked me to stand up so that he could examine my back. He then asked me to bend over at the waist (this was very uncomfortable). He said that things looked a lot worse than the last time he saw me and that he may have to put more metal work into the spine than he first thought. He decides that rather than send me back for more x-rays, he would on the day of my operation stretch me to see if it was the same. He said it would be too painful to do it at the moment and added that he would do it when I was taken into theartre. He is concerned at how much my spine had worsened.

How Mr. Oxborrow hopes to go about the operation:
Mr. Oxborrow explained that the incision would be made down my side; he would deflate my lungs and might have to remove a rib in order to reach the spine. He would also need to detach the diaphragm to gain access to the spine and remove the disc material from between the vertebra involved in the curve. This would increase the flexibility of the curve and provide a large surface area for spinal fusion. Rods would be put in place from the side. He told me the spine could go worse doing it this way. But if it were his daughter he would want to try this way first, I was a little worried about this. But I guess the doctor knows best and I had lots of trust in him.

Talks About the risk and complications:
Mr. Oxborrow explained that doing spinal surgery is major surgery and the operation would take all day. I will not go into this too much because it's all very scary. But some of the risks are; chest infection, due to drains in the lungs after surgery, thrombosis (blood clots) to lungs due to him deflating the lungs and to the legs due to not being able to get out of bed. One leg may feel cold and the other warm (this can last for many months). Also because I had been in a brace for so long the

spine may decide it didn't like its new shape when they try to straighten it and go into spasm in which case they have to stop surgery.

Mr. Oxborrow explained there was a chance that I could be paralysed as a result of the operation and that there was also a chance that I might not survive the operation. Throughout the operation the technologist would monitor my spinal cord to make sure it was not being damaged. If things looked to be going wrong I would be woken up mid-operation and asked to wriggle my toes to check that my spinal cord hadn't been damaged. But these are very rare problems. But he said he had to tell me the risk involved with the surgery I was about to have.

Surgery was going to be made more difficult because I am skinny (so my doctor told me). Mr. Oxborrow explained that the surgery was going to be very demanding on my body so being a good weight would help in my recovery.

The rods used to support my spine would be titanium rods and would be fixed in place with screws, wire and hooks.

How I am feeling at the moment:
When my surgeon said that I needed surgery to correct my curved spine (scoliosis), going back a few years ago, I felt a little scared about having surgery. Having spinal surgery was a big decision for me to make. However, I was trying to look at the positive sides of having my curved spine straightened. I was trying to keep a positive attitude towards what I was about to go through and how much better off I would be in later life. My lengthened, straighter trunk would increase my overall height and eliminate the long term need for a back brace. My sitting posture would be greatly improved. I knew everything would be ok, I have family and friends and they are all very supportive, plus I had the number one spinal doctor doing the operation.

16th February 2005:
Time for me to donate 1 unit of blood, I'm off to have a thumb prick done first Waaaaaaaaa, I remember this from last time. I think I was very brave, mum held my hand and the nurse gives me a nice badge (told you I was brave). I am also given a white box, which looks, like a small ice cooler into which my bag of blood will go to keep it cool.

Back to the clinic to give my unit of blood, I had to wait for a while so Scott, my teddy and I went and played with this car, which was a transformer one that turned into a robot! Then we made a jigsaw puzzle. By this time it was my turn, I tried to hide Waaaaaaaa. The nurse checked my blood pressure and temperature and completed some necessary paperwork.

I had to lie on a bed, the EMLA cream, which my mum had put on my arm about an hour earlier, was removed and a needle put into the vein for the replacement fluid, the needle was BIG! And inserted into my little arm, it stung a bit but not as much as the thumb prick. Then the needle used to collect the blood was inserted, this one really, really hurt Waaaaaa and went straight through a vein. The blood was collected in a donor bag and it took about 30 minutes. After the donation was complete the needles were removed and a dressing applied. I had to rest for about 15 minutes; I was also given a Mars bar and a can of coke to boost my sugar level. I had to rest for the rest of the day.

18th February 2005:
I went for my Electroencephalogram (EEG) a nerve conduction test; this only took about 20 minutes. I had to lie on a bed and small discs were placed on my scalp and feet with a sticky paste (poor nurse having to touch my feet). They had wires attached to pads. I then felt small electrical pulses which activate the nerves and were felt as a tapping. The activity of my brain was recorded for a few minutes. The test was slightly uncomfortable but not painful. The technologist told me they would be in theatre during the surgery on the spine to help the surgeon make sure nerves were not damaged during the operation.

Family care worker:
I also met Sandra the family care worker. She was really nice. Sandra showed me round the ward I would be going on. She introduced me to some of the nurses and told mum they would try and give her a parents' room or a bed next to me. She also took me down to the I.C.U Unit but I did not go in, Sandra decided it may be a bit scary for me and I would not remember being on there anyway. We gave each other a big hug and she wished me luck and said she would come and see me. The day I was to be admitted for surgery.

9th March 2005 the day before my operation:

During the late afternoon, I went into Pendlebury Children's hospital to prepare for my surgery the next day. But first I was asked to go in to school so that I could be presented with a special award in our school assembly (The Diana, Princess of Wales Memorial Award). I was presented with a special certificate and a lapel pin badge. My head Teacher (Mr. Peter Brooks) and Mr. Ridley nominated me for the award. I was the first pupil at the college to receive the Diana Princess of Wales Memorial Award for commitment and work in numerous fields, including fundraising for the " When You Wish Upon A Star" charity. I was in the press and my head teacher gave the following statement:

Head teacher, Peter Brooks, said: "Kirsty is a super student and a great ambassador for the school."I was delighted to be able to present Kirsty with the award. She thoroughly deserves this national recognition. "In school, Kirsty is a very hard working, fun loving student who fulfils her study as a prefect impeccably. Out of school Kirsty works tirelessly raising money for the 'Wish upon a Star' charity and supporting other children who have suffered from illnesses similar to her own." Kirsty first became involved with "When You Wish Upon A Star" when she took part in the children's charity's annual trip to Lapland at the age of nine.

Mr. Brooks, said: "Since she went on that visit she has worked herself tirelessly to send children on the trip she went on. She's an amazing kid. She gets involved in everything yet she spends her life wearing a body brace. Her work has included organising cake sales and bric-a-bracs".

Mr. Brooks is a cool teacher and makes it a pleasure to attend his school.

My First day in hospital:

When I arrived on the ward I was made welcome by the nurses, I was shown to my bed and introduced to the other children on the ward. There was one other girl in the bay who had had the same operation as I was about to have and one girl who was about to go home. They keep the spinal children separate from the main ward due to risk of infection. There are only three children in the spinal bay at any one time.

Dr. Tarek (one of my surgeon) came to see me and explained what was going to happen the next day. He told me to try and get good nights kip and that Mr. Oxborrow would be down to see me early in the morning before I went to theatre. Next I had a visit from the physiotherapist who explained that I would have a chest drain in my chest after surgery and that she would come and see me again after surgery. My dad went home about 9.00pm and said he would be back very early in the morning. I settled down about 11.00pm, mum was just about to kip on the chair next to my bed when one of the nurses told mum to jump in the other empty bed as no other children could come in this bay.

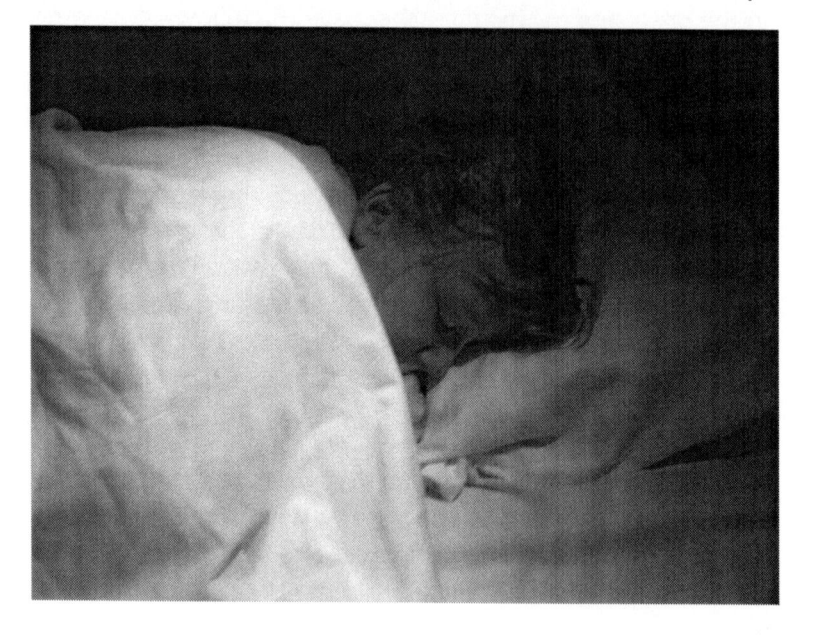

Settled and sleeping night before my operation

Kirsty's Story

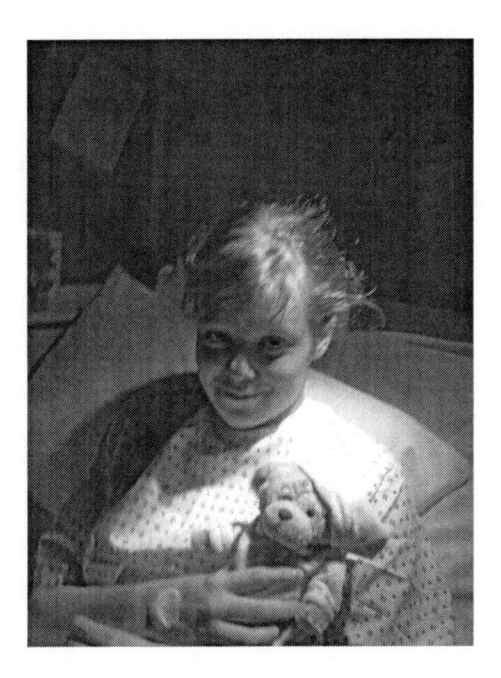

10th March 2005: The day of my operation:
I was woken really early by "Sam" one of the nurses. Mum had just got back from having a shower.

Mr. Oxborrow (my surgeon), and his team came to see me soon after and tried to calm me (they did a good job); next Dylon (the anastetist) came and ran through things with me (he is really nice and very funny). My dad turned up next, I was asked to change into my operating gown, and a nurse put cream on the backs of my hands. These two ladies came to do the nerve impulse test. They stuck electrodes on my head and ankles and linked the wires coming from them to a machine, which was then linked to a computer. I then sat on my bed and had to stay as relaxed as possible. From the computer she sent a pulse into my ankles. It's a bit like pins and needles. The computer then recorded the signal going up my spine into my brain. This test is so that during the operation they could compare my normal signal to all the signals they get during the operation. It means that they can detect if a nerve is affected. There is absolutely NO pain involved!! The wires are left in place for when I am in theatre.

I was wheeled from the Liebert ward down to the operating theatre, which was next to ICU and HDU, with mum, dad and a nurse walking at the side of me. It was only now that I started to feel a bit scared. When we reached the theatre only mum and the nurse were allowed in with me. We went through some doors to get to the theatre room. The room smelt funny, they would not let dad in as the room was only small and they needed the room so they could move round. Mum had to put some plastic coverings on her shoes.

Mr. Oxborrow came out to see me and asked if I was ok and if I would like to look in the room where the operation was going to take place. I said "Yes" so he sat me up and opened the door, I could see lots of machines. The room was brightly lit and looked really clean. I could see a trolley draped with a green cloth that had lots of surgical instruments laid out on it.

The anesthetists (Dylon) came and said "Hi" then stuck these sticky pads on my chest, which would monitor my heart rate during the operation. Mum squeezed my hand and looked at me with clear unblinking eyes, I could tell my mum was fighting back the tears. But her voice stayed strong and mum said she loved me and wished she could take my place. I was then given an injection and asked to count, I don't know what number I got to, everything went so quickly. I hardly remember them putting me to sleep, as I was talking to my mum and I had my new teddy, which Kat from Post Pal sent me.

Operation is stopped:
I remember Mr. Oxborrow saying to mum that she could ask one of the nurses on the ward to phone the theatre at any time to ask how the surgery was going.

I'll let mum tell you what happened while I was in theatre as I was in the land of nod and stayed pretty much out it for the next four days.

Kirsty's Story

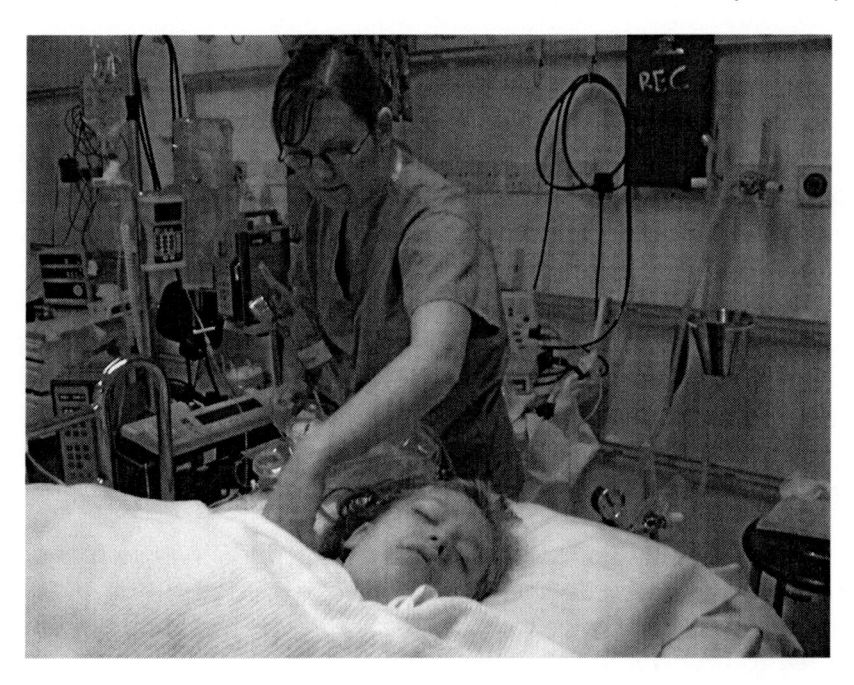

Kirsty in H.D.U

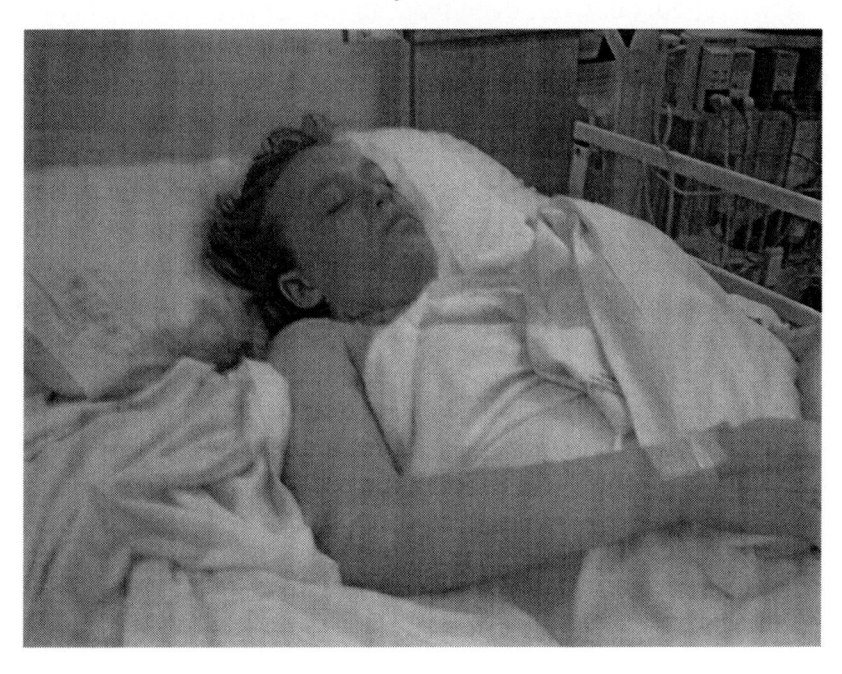

Kirsty Ashton

Mum:
I tried really hard not to get upset; I don't want you to see me cry. I give you a kiss and hold your hand until you fall asleep. You are now in their hands for the next 12 hours. Your dad and I go for a brew and just wait not really knowing what to do for the next twelve hours. This is so difficult. Every minute seems like ten, and we just walk the corridors of the hospital in a daze not even able to talk to each other. We decided to go back to the ward and wait for news. Twelve hours is a long time and I am trying really hard to keep strong but I can't help thinking about what Mr. Oxborrow said to me and all the risk involved in the surgery. I pray to God everything will be ok. I keep getting text from family and friends' asking how things are going. Everyone is so worried about you.

At about 4.30pm we decided to ask one of the nurses to find out how you are doing. So she rings the theatre to find out for us. We are told things are going to plan and that he will be at least another three to four hours before he is finished. We decide to go to the canteen for a drink, and we tell the nurse where we will be incase we are needed. I had not even finished my drink when a call comes through to the canteen asking for Mr. and Mrs. Ashton to return to the Liebert ward. I froze in my seat; your dad grabs my hand and squeezes it tight, and walks me back to your ward. We were met by one of the nurses who said that Mr. Oxborrow wanted to see us outside the theatre (this is not looking good); I looked at your dad and said "what's gone wrong?" I'm so nervous and as we approached the theatre Mr. Oxborrow came out to see us. He was looking worried (I could not holdback the tears: believe me I did try). He told us that he had to stop the operation due to complications and that he would have to try and complete the operation in a few days when he has looked at the situation again. He said that he had woken you mid surgery and asked you to wriggle your toes and that you were unable to move them, which was causing some worry. But he didn't think you would remember him waking you.

Mr. Oxborrow asked me if I wanted him to tell you that you will need to go back to surgery or do I want to do it. I felt it best if we told you.

Kirsty's Story

We were taken to the recovery room where you were attached to so many machines. A nurse stood over you, as I went to give you a hug and tell you that the operation had been stopped before it should have been. You told me that Mr. Oxborrow had woken you and asked you to wriggle your toes and that you couldn't move them. You said you were not in any pain when Mr. Oxborrow woke you.

You were then taken to H.D.U (high dependence unit); you had tubes and wires coming out from all over the place.

Mr. Oxborrow came back to see you and asked again if you could move your toes, which you were still unable to do.

Mr. Oxborrow said that he was going to phone another doctor who trained him and ask him for some advice as his daughter also has NF and he would know what to do next. He was really concerned with what happened in surgery.

Mr. Oxborrow explained that it was very important that you were only log rolled until you have your next operation (this would take five nurse's) It was very important that you did not try to sit up due to your spine being so unstable and remember you did not have the rods in place yet.

By now it was getting really late. I was not allowed to stay with you over night while you were on H.D.U as the nurse needed room to get round your bed (I had been given a parents room). I made sure you were comfortable before kissing you on the head and going back to my room to let people know what had happened and try and get some sleep. Your dad went home. I managed to doze through sheer exhaustion. As I fell in and out of sleep, thoughts of what had happened the day before and knowing you had got to go through it all again swirled through my mind. It was hard to see you in so much pain. Monitors kept bleeping and the nurses kept running in to you. You have been really sick during the night and managed to get it all over the nurses, so when I got to H.D.U in the morning the nurses were sat in different uniforms telling me that they had to change after you had been so sick.

Kirsty Ashton

The staff nurse tells me you were restless. You kept grabbing at your oxygen mask they gave you because you were finding it hard to breathe.

Your mouth was really dry and you wanted a drink but all we could give you was a damp swab, which you could suck on to wet your mouth. You kept falling asleep. You were given anti-sickness medicine but none of them worked and you continued being really sick. After a couple of days you had the chest drain taken out. You were really very brave and coped with this well even though it was painful but it was so quick that it didn't really matter. After four days on H.D.U you were taken back to the main ward while you waited for the second operation. Mr. Oxborrow called everyday to see you and some times twice. He was still very concerned by what had happened. I was worried about you going back to the ward. You really didn't look ready. You were still being sick and in a lot of pain. But they needed the bed (only 4 beds on the unit). Mr. Oxborrow said he would be happier if you stayed on H.D.U too. You still could not move your toes, which was causing a lot of worry.

Back on my ward:
I was still in a lot of pain and attached to drips and other machines, I was not allowed to move or sit up and to be honest I couldn't if I tried. It took five nurse to log roll me when my bed was being changed. My next operation was now scheduled for the following Thursday.

Mr. Oxborrow came and sat on the side of my bed. He told me he would not be able to do the operation as he had to be somewhere else, I got really upset and looked over at mum, I told him I did not want anyone else to do my operation. The only person I wanted to do my surgery, was him. Mr. Oxborrow has many letters after his name to testify he is one of the best at what he does.

Mr. Oxborrow must have realised how upset I was by the news I had just been given for he said, "Ok. I will cancel all my other appointments to be there for you." (How nice was that). Not long after I took a turn for the worse and started being really sick and my temperature was high.

Mr. Oxborrow called to see me on the morning of my surgery just to go over things with me again. Mum mentioned she was worried that

Kirsty's Story

I was still being sick and that my temperature was so high. He asked the nurse to pass him my chart and after reading the chart he was not happy that no one had informed him that my condition had worsened. He took my temperature, which was 38.6 so he asked for a fan to be put on my locker to try and get the temperature down and gave me 10ml of paracetamol, but I was sick soon after taking it, I couldn't have any more, because the doctor was not sure how much I had absorbed. Then looking down at my catheter he said it looked like I might have a urine infection so told one of the nurses to take a sample and said that he wanted an urgent lab test done and results back within the next 30 minutes.

Results came back and he was right, I did have an infection. I was put on antibiotics and the operation had to be postponed and planned again for the Monday. Yet again Mr. Oxborrow was meant to be somewhere else but knowing I did not want anyone else to do the surgery he promised me he would be there for me.

I felt really bad that Mr. Oxborrow had cancelled all his other appointments and apologized to him. He told me not to be daft and to just concentrate on getting better.

I was still unable to sit up and my hair was a mess, I still had all the sticky stuff in it from where I had had the electrodes pads stuck on my head. Some of my friends from school were coming to visit me and I wanted my hair washing. But because I could not move this was a real difficult task. But it really did need doing so one of the nurses moved my bed forward so she could get behind it and mum put a bowl on the floor and sheet under my head. One of the other nurses held my head and neck and another nurse poured the water over my hair, then shampoo, with my hair being so long it took over 45 minutes. Mum then blow-dried it for me, I felt so much better for having my hair washed. Mum put it in a plait to keep it tidy.

My friends stayed for a while giving me all the gossip that was going on in school, like who was now going out with whom and who's finished with whom. It gave mum a chance to go and relax and have a cuppa with my friend's mum who incidentally mum knows.

Kirsty Ashton

The drip in my arm kept bleeping; the cannula in my hand was causing problems as usual so the doctor was called to have it resited.

My friends told me that Mr. Brooks (my head teacher) had been keeping the students informed on how I was doing in the school assembly and that the other morning everyone thought I died (charming) as Mr. Brooks had announced there had been a problem during surgery. It was the way in which he built up to saying it that made everyone think the worse. Some of the students were crying by the news.

Monday, time to try again
Mr. Oxborrow came to see me really early, with another doctor who said to me "I believe you don't want me to do your surgery" and I replied "Correct" so he said "That's ok, I'll go and play a round golf" so I told him to enjoy his day on the golf course.

Mr. Oxborrow took my temperature, which was 36.8, and was happy for the operation to go ahead, he said that he would see me later in theatre. About an hour later I started being unwell, I was still taken to theatre where Mr. Oxborrow was waiting for me. He took one look at me and said he was not happy with the way I looked and took my temperature: bad news my temperature had gone to 37.9. He said "I'm sorry Kirsty I cannot take the chance with a temperature that high" and I was sent back to the ward. The other parents and kids on the ward started cheering when they saw me being wheeled back and could not believe it. More antibiotics were given to try and get rid of the infection and my temperature was taken every two hours for the next two days. Mr. Oxborrow said he wanted it to stay below 37.4 for 48 hours before he could go ahead with the operation. The Operation was then planned for Thursday.

Tuesday 23rd March 2005:
I had been getting some pain in my leg and mentioned it to my mum, who gave my leg a rub to try and make me feel better but as mum rubbed her hand down my leg she felt three lumps and asked me how long had the lumps been there. Unable to answer, mum told one of the nurses who came and had a look at my leg and decided to call one of the doctors to look at my leg. The doctor came within minutes and was also puzzled by the lumps so called for a second opinion. No one was really sure what they were and suggested that it could be from where I

Kirsty's Story

had been having needles. Mr. Oxborrow was told of the situation when he came to do his ward round the next day. Mr. Oxborrow ordered an ultrasound scan to be done of my leg and as I was still not allowed to sit up I was wheeled down to the x-ray department on my bed. It was a bit of a struggle getting the bed into the scan room but the doctor managed it in the end.

I watched the scan on a screen as the doctor scanned over my leg, I could see three large lumps in my leg. Still unsure what they were at this point the results of the scan were passed on to Mr. Oxborrow who came to see me and explained that I did have three lumps in my leg and that he wanted me to have an MRI scan of my leg and for me to see an oncologist for a second opinion. I did not know what the job of oncologist was at the time; to me it was just another doctor. But I remember mum went white when she heard the words "oncologist". I never thought anymore about it. I have since learnt that an Oncologist doctor specialises in the treatment of cancer, which is why my mum went white at the time.

I was in a lot of pain and still being very sick but I never got the chance to be down as the nurses were always around cheering you up and making you laugh. One night, we got the nurses to play the "YES", "NO" game. What a laugh. A lot of your fellow patients are having the same operation so you can help each other through any tough times too. Those friendships you make are precious.

Thursday, 24th March 2005:
Mr. Oxborrow called to see me to make sure I was feeling ok for surgery, The nurses and doctors were very reassuring that everything would be ok this time and my parents were there for me every step of the way so I didn't really have too much to worry about with surgery. After making sure there was an empty bed on H.D.U I was prepared for surgery, and cream put on the back of my hand.

Mr. Oxborrow explained that he would be doing the posterior approach this time, which was done, from the back of the body. It involves making a long, straight incision into my back and moving aside the back muscles to reveal my spine.

Kirsty Ashton

He would then insert two titanium rods, holding the rods in place with wires, hooks, and screws at various points. The spine would be repositioned and held in place with these mechanisms while the new bone surface fused. Mr. Oxborrow said he would need to do a bone graft, so bone will be taken from my pelvic bone. This would help the spinal bones fuse together in a permanent position.

Mr. Oxborrow explained that the surgical risks involved were the same as before.

During my first operation the approach for my scoliosis surgery was done through an incision from the side of the body. This technique is better for severe curves, including rigid curves in adults, but has greater surgical risks than posterior surgery.

Time for the nerve impulse electrodes to be stuck to my head, which was done so the doctors could detect if a nerve was affected during the operation, which is what happened on my first operation. There was absolutely no pain involved!! Getting the glue out of my long hair after is the worse part about having this done. I was given a little tip to use nail varnish to try and remove the glue when I felt up to having my hair washed. Believe me, it did help.

I remember going into theatre and talking with Mr. Oxborrow. He was reassuring me everything would be ok and I was confident I was in safe hands with Mr. Oxborrow.

I will let my mum tell you what happens while I am in theatre as I was in cuckoo land for the next few hours.

Both John and I were with Kirsty as she went down for surgery and as before they would not let your dad into the anaesthetic room. As Kirsty grabbed my hand and squashed it really tight I felt a lump in my throat, I was even more scared this time due to what happened on your last operation. I wanted to shout for them to stop but knew the operation had to be done. I was so worried at the time. There were so many emotions whirling around inside my head.

Mr. Oxborrow puts his hand on my shoulder and promised me he would look after you and told me to get one of the nurses to phone the theatre anytime I wanted an up date to how things were going. I

Kirsty's Story

gave you a kiss on your head as you nodded off to sleep, told you how much we all love you and that we would see you very soon.

Mr. Oxborrow told me not to worry and that he would see me later. The nurse led me out of the anasetic room where your dad was waiting. We give each other a hug and went for a drink in the canteen and for the next eight hours we just sat around not really knowing what to say or do.

Hours later the nurse told us the operation was over and that Mr. Oxborrow was waiting to see us at the theatre. This time Mr. Oxborrow had a smile on his face so everything had been successful. We were both led to the recovery room before you were moved to the HDU ward. You tried to say "Hi" but you were too sleepy, I gave you a kiss and said we would see you on the ward when the nurse's had settled you down.

I remember seeing mum, dad and Mr. Oxborrow looking over me asking if I was ok. I felt a bit weird, I wasn't allowed a drink for hours and I was really thirsty. I kept being asked to wiggle my toes. I was wheeled to H.D.U and after a while the nurse and my mum put water on my lips and in my mouth with a swab as my lips were so dry. The next day I had an x-ray machine brought over to me and a board slid underneath me so they could take an x-ray of my spine, which was a bit uncomfortable. They removed the board and put my x-ray up on a screen in front of me. Mr. Oxborrow said he was really pleased at the results and pointed out where he had to hook over the top of my rib because he could not get a screw into the spine to hold the rods. I was then told to rest. I kept falling asleep. I was given different anti-sickness medicine, but none of them worked I kept on being really sick, this is only to be expected after such big surgery.

Mum said she was off to my ward to let them know how I was doing, while dad stayed with me. When mum came back I could not believe who she had with her, I thought I was seeing things, she had Danny Young with her (Warren out of Corrie') and Nikki Sanderson (who played Candice Stowe in Corrie'). I was not looking or feeling my best, my face was swollen and I had just been sick but it really made my day seeing Danny. He stayed for a little while chatting and gave me a little hug. I wanted to hug him back but I could not move.

Kirsty Ashton

I have decided to let mum tell you about Danny's visit as I didn't remember everything, which I am still sad about.

Mum:
I decided to go and let the nurses and your friends on the ward know how the operation went as they were all waiting for news, I was told Danny Young (Warren out of Correnation St') and Nikki Sanderson (Candice out of Correnation St') were in the hospital, I knew how much you really loved Danny Young as you had many posters of him up on your bedroom wall. I was talking with some friends on the corridor of the hospital when Danny came up to me and said "Hello Babe" (I could not believe it). I told him about you being on H.D.U and how poorly you had been. Danny asked where you were so that he could visit you. Nikki was running up behind him asking him where he was going and he said "I'm off to see Kirsty", Nikki said that she wanted to come and see Kirsty too.

Danny and Nikki were both very upset when they saw how poorly you were and one of the nurses (Lesley) heard that Danny had gone to see you and she came running up to H.D.U to see your face. You really were not very well at the time and your face was swollen and you were in a lot of pain. But that did not matter; Danny and Nikki were really nice and made your day. They could see how poorly you were and decided to leave so I walked them back out of the HDU and on to the main corridor. Danny gave me a hug. He was really upset after seeing you and we chatted for about ten minutes. Before Danny left he asked me if you had a mobile phone and if he could have your number as he wanted to keep in contact with you. He then gave me his mobile number and asked me to pass it onto you when you were feeling a little better. I think you thought I was having you on when I went back and told you that I had Danny's mobile number for you. But you had a little twinkle in your eyes, which made me smile.

Soon after mum got back I fell asleep. When I woke I was in some pain and started being sick so I was given some morphine and anti sickness medicine.

I don't know what time it was but mum went to the parents' room for some much needed rest. My drip had stopped working and I had to have it replaced with another in my wrist, I remember getting upset, I wanted the nurse to phone my mum. But the nurses told me that my mum needed a rest and would not call her, I understood mum needed a rest but I so much wanted my mum, I just wanted a hug from her. When mum came in the next morning I told her I wanted her in the night. Mum got upset that she was not there for me and we gave each other a big hug.

Danny Young visits Kirsty on the H.D.U

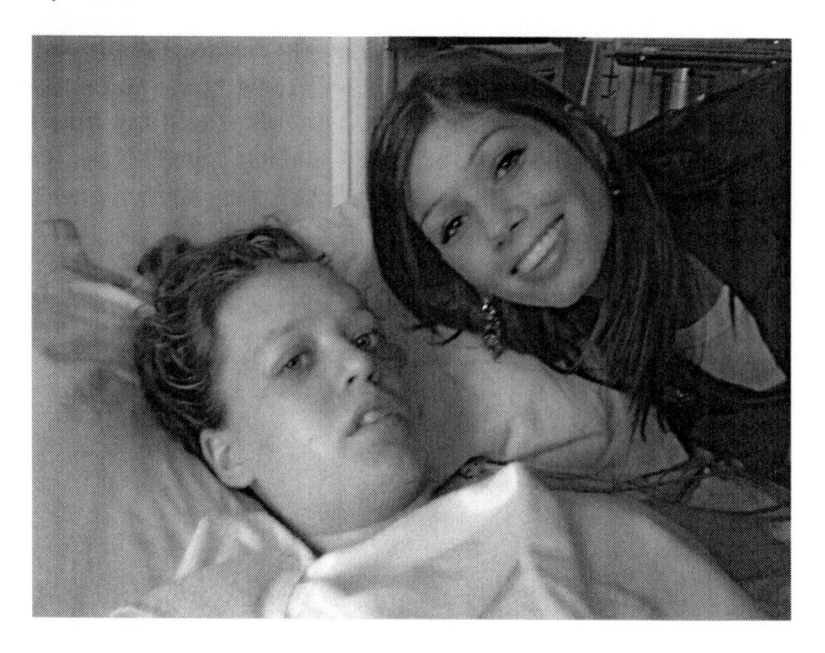

Kirsty Ashton

Nikki Sanderson visits Kirsty on H.D.U

I had my chest drain removed this morning so I feel a little more comfortable. The surgeon had to put a chest drain in my chest during the operation because he had collapsed my lungs so that he could get to the spine. I still had numerous other tubes in me and I'm still being sick but I am able to be moved back to my ward (Liebert).

Back on the ward:
The operation was over and I started on the road to recovery.

After a couple of days the catheter was removed. This just felt a little uncomfortable but was not painful. I had not been out of bed for over three weeks and about seven days after my second surgery the physiotherapist decided that it was time to see if I could sit up on the side of my bed, I needed to be fitted for my new spinal brace. This was my first time of sitting up in 3 weeks. I used this special technique. I rolled onto my side and then swung my legs off the side of my bed while sitting up. It made me feel sick and dizzy sitting up for the first time in three weeks but I was pleased to be able to do it. I had to have two nurse's and my mum help hold me up while Clair wrapped wet plaster round me and this other guy smoothed it to make the mould for the brace. Unfortunately I started being sick and had to be given an

Kirsty's Story

injection to try and stop it. Clair told me my Brace would be ready on the 5th April (My Birthday). The next day I sat in the chair for a couple of minutes. My nurse stayed by me and so did my mum, I felt really dizzy and sick and could only manage a few minutes before I had to go back to bed. The following day I did the same. I was going to try and stand up but I didn't feel confident enough, my legs felt like jelly all wobbly, so I didn't.

The following day I managed to stand up. I walked a couple of steps also. It felt uncomfortable as all the muscles had to adjust but I knew as soon as I got up and about the better I would get.

The day after that I walked a bit and sat in the chair for a couple of minutes. By now I was starting to get the hang of it and I was gaining more and more confidence. I just wished this sickness would stop.

The nurses and other medical staff were simply brilliant. They are so in tune with teens and young adults they help you feel relaxed. A lot of effort had been taken to make not only patients, but also relatives and friends feel as comfortable as possible. Open visiting, TVs by the beds and DVDs and computer games to borrow. I believe it is so important to try to lead as normal life as possible and remain as independent as your situation permits while in hospital.

5th April 2005 My 15th Birthday:
I received lots of cards and gifts from family, friends and hospital staff and I had a large box of gifts from my friends at Post pal.

My friends on the ward organised a surprise party for me and Julie Hesmondhalgh (Haley out of Coronation St") and Ian Kershaw (Julie's husband) came to see me. They both sprang onto the ward singing "Happy Birthday" and they looked really funny. While Julie and Ian were with me the nurses wheeled in this great big cake with more gifts from all the children and staff on the ward. I could not have candles on the cake due to the oxygen at the side of my bed so Julie took the cake to the door and put one on for me so I could blow out the candle at the door. I had a really nice day and even if I was in hospital everyone tried to make it very special for me. Clair called with my new brace all wrapped up in a big bow and my doctors called and sang happy birthday to me.

Kirsty Ashton

Danny Young phoned to wish me happy birthday, I couldn't believe it I didn't even know mum had told him when my birthday was. It really cheered me up to hear from Danny.

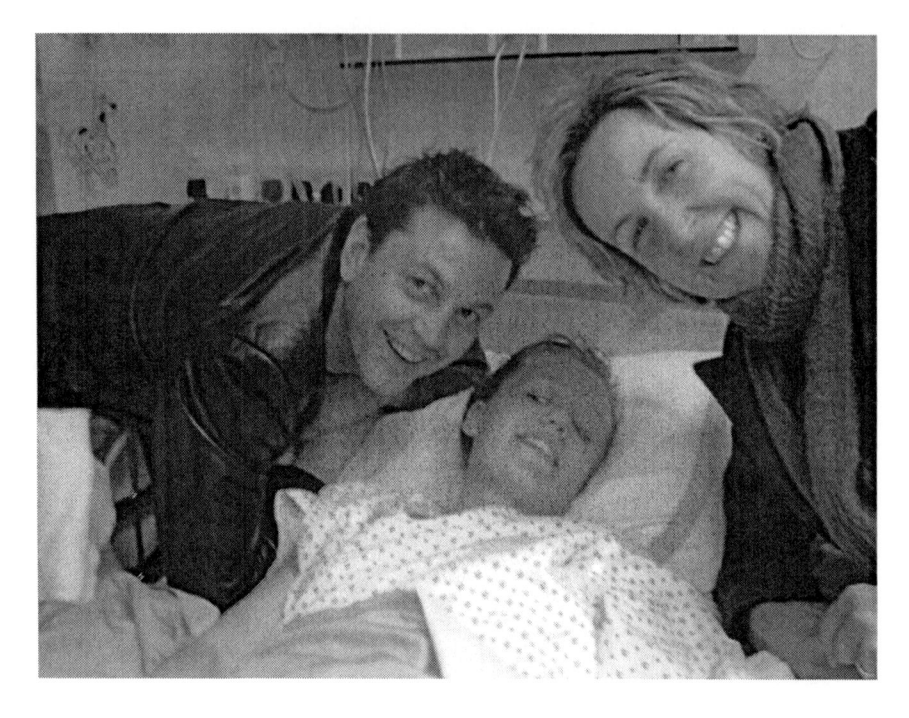

Julie Hesmondhalgh and Ian Kershaw visit Kirsty on her Birthday

Kirsty's Story

6th April 2005:
I had to go and see the oncologist doctor over the results of the scan I had done on my leg. One of the nurses wheeled me down to the clinic in my wheelchair as I could not walk very far due to the pain I was still getting in my legs and back. I was called in to see the doctor and mum and the nurse came in the room with me. The doctor was really scary and never smiled all the time she was talking to me. She explained she had looked at the scan reports and felt that the tumours in my leg were nothing to worry about unless they started to grow above 5cm in which case they should be removed.

Getting ready for going home:
A couple of days before I went home, I went down to the x-ray department, to have two standing x-rays taken. I was wheeled down in a wheelchair because I could not stand up very well without feeling dizzy. I was still very weak after losing so much weight and still feeling very sick.

X-Ray:
Mr. Oxborrow brought the x-rays to show me and explained that he had inserted two titanium rods down either side of my spine and pins and hooks to hold the rods to the spine. He pointed out everything in detail on the x-ray for me. I am so glad he played with Meccano when he was younger...ha..ha.. It looks like he did a great job.

Mr. Oxborrow extracted the sacks of fluid that everyone has between each vertebra and then fused each vertebra together to make my spine solid. He also used bone from my pelvis for the bone graft.

8th April 2005: Home at last
I know I had only been away from home for a few weeks but I felt really strange walking into the house. During the night I had been up being really sick and my poor mum got no sleep as she was constantly checking on me. The next day I continued being sick and when mum took my temperature it was 38.7 so mum decided it best if she phoned the ward and the nurse said she would ring mum back in a few minutes after she had spoken to the doctor. Mum was asked to bring me back to the hospital, I had to be readmitted with sickness and a high temperature. After being checked over by the doctor I was allowed home again on the Sunday on some new tablets and given an appointment to see Mr. Oxborrow on the Friday.

Friday and time to see Mr. Oxborrow:
I was still feeling very unwell and by the time I reached the hospital I could hardly stand up, I felt so dizzy and sick, Mr. Oxborrow saw me straight away and did not like the look of me and phoned his medical team to ask them to have a look at me. I was taken over to the acute unit where I started being really sick I was kept in hospital for more tests.

Kirsty's Story

A few hours later I was moved over to Sullivan ward. My temperature was still high and even though I was given an injection to stop the sickness I was still being sick so I was put back on the drip to try and get some fluid back into me.

Mum stayed with me and slept on a reclining chair next to my bed. Mum said she did not want a bed over in the parents' room as it meant her walking across an unlit car park at night to get to the parents' room and she did not feel safe doing so.

When I was on the Liebert ward before the parents room was only down the corridor and mum would sit with me until I fell a sleep, sometimes as late as 1am when mum would go to her room, which she often shared with the parents of other sick children and she would try and get some sleep before getting up again at 6.30am so she could be with me for when I woke up at 7.30am.

Mum did not expect me to be in hospital for as long as I was, which was another reason for my mum not wanting a parents' room.

The following day Mr. Oxborrow called to see me on the ward and was not pleased to see me looking so poorly and wanted me to have an Ultrasound scan to make sure I did not have a blood clot in my tummy from when I had the spinal surgery. I was still being sick and hadn't eaten anything for days, I was also finding it hard to drink so Mr. Oxborrow said the drip must stay up until I was able to keep fluids down. Ultrasounds scan use's sound waves to build up a picture of the inside of the body. They are completely painless. The test did not really confirm anything fortunately, no blood clots were seen.

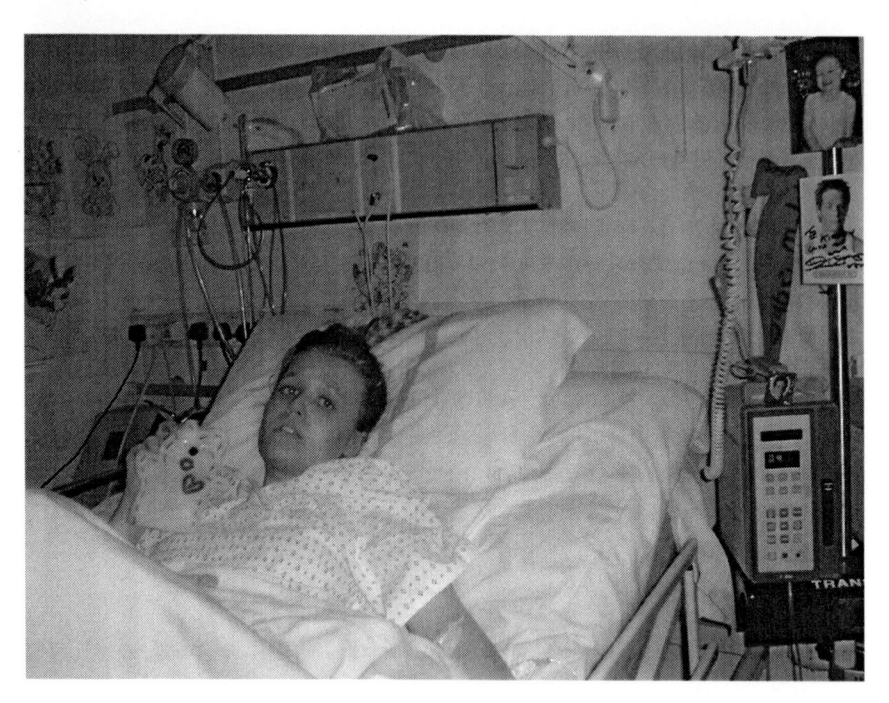

May 2005: Test, which Was done over the following weeks:
Over the next few weeks things were not getting any better, I continued to be sick and I was losing weight.

A few days later I was told I would be having an endoscope test, this is where the doctor can look in side the stomach and take a biopsy of the lining of the stomach if they feel it's necessary to do so.

I was going to be transferred to Booth Hall Children's Hospital for the endoscope test but the doctor said I was not well enough to be moved so the doctor from Booth Hall came to me.

On the morning of the tests I was wheeled over to the main hospital operating theatre as the endoscope test was being done under a general anaesthetic. The anaesthetist stuck the sticky pads on my chest to monitor my heart rate. He tried to give me an injection but was having problems finding a vein, I had had so many injections that my veins kept collapsing. He then tried to place a gas mask over my mouth and nose and he told me it would smell of chocolate, I began to struggle as I felt as though I could not breathe. I must have fallen asleep because I can't remember much after that. Mum told me that a long flexible tube that had a camera and light on the end of it was put down into my stomach. The doctor took samples (biopsies) of some tissues through the endoscope so he could look at it more closely under a microscope and look for this bug (Helicobacter Pylori) that had shown up in all my blood tests. Helicobacter Pylori is a bacteria that causes chronic inflammation of the inner lining of the stomach,

Mum was called to theatre while I was in recovery and the doctor explained to mum that my stomach lining was very inflamed and my food was not moving across correctly and any food that I ate was just building up causing me to be sick. I was put on two new tablets, (I can't remember what the first tablet was called but one of them was called Omeprazole) to see if they would help take the inflammation in my tummy down. It would be a week before he got the results of the biopsy back.

I was moved on to another ward while I recovered from the anaesthetic. It must have been about 11.00pm when I started being really sick again and my temperature went up to 38.9. The nurse bleeped the on call doctor as she was getting worried. The doctor stayed with me for about an hour and resited the drip in my arm. I was given paracetamol and a fan was placed on my locker to try and bring the temperature down. Late on the next day I was moved back to my ward on my bed. The move across the car park was a bit bumpy.

Brain scan
I kept getting some really bad headaches, I think it was due to how hot and stuffy it was in the hospital. But the doctor ordered a brain scan just to make sure that there had been no change to the tumour near the brain stem. The results came back and everything looked to be ok and confirmed that I still had a brain.

A PH Study:
Doctors decided to do a PH Study, which measures the acid that refluxes from the stomach. All medication was stopped for about 24 hours before the test was scheduled to begin.

A very thin tube thinner than a feeding tube was inserted up my nostril until it reached just above my stomach, It had a very small probe at the end that registered any acids that were refluxed from my stomach. The nurse asked me to drink some water as this makes it easier for the end of the tube to travel to the oesophagus. Inserting the tube does not hurt but it is really uncomfortable while they are doing it. It can take more than one attempt to insert the tube, which happened with me. It also made me sneeze, I also kept retching because it was tickling the back of my throat and made my eyes water. When the tube had been inserted, the nurse put some tape on my cheek to hold it in place. An x-ray was taken to make sure that the probe has been positioned correctly. The other end of the thin tube was attached to a small computer (In my case a small black box) for 24 hours.

Meanwhile I was given a diary sheet to complete, which has to be a running history. You state the time of each activity that takes place whilst the study is being done and when you are feeling sick or eating and having a drink. I was so glad when my 24 hours were up I really did not like having the tube up my nostril. I got my test results back a few days later and everything was ok.

Although all this was happening to me, I think it was worse for my mum having to watch me go through it all.

When the doctors did their ward round in the mornings they stayed at my bedside just long enough to say "Hello". I kept watching other children coming and going and kept asking when I could go home, but all I got from the doctors were friendly smiles and no other comments made.

Miss Hill my drama teacher from school came to visit me; she told me all the news that was happening at school, which was great to hear.

Before I came into hospital I had been part of the Young Enterprise scheme with some friends at school where we had to set up a business for an academic year. Through the Young Enterprise scheme, we had complete control of our own company. We made and sold cards, book marks and other stationery items Young Enterprise offers an invaluable experience of business management, developing our skills in teamwork and co-operation, and you learn to succeed by working together to achieve a common goal. We were also given the chance to compete in local, national and even international competitions and to take part in regional trade fairs. Miss Hill told me that I had been put forward

Kirsty's Story

for the young achiever of the year Award, which was part of the Young Enterprise scheme and she came to tell me that I had won. But the presentation was to take place two days later and as I was still in hospital one of my friends was going along to pick my award up for me and bring it to the hospital for me.

June 2005:
Into June and I was still in hospital, doctor still don't know why I was still being so sick and losing weight. My dietitian decided I should have Polycal in my foods and drinks as well as the Scandishakes in the hope I would put some weight on. If not I would have to have a nasal gastric tube put in (I sure hoped not). Polycal is used for special medical purposes and for dietary management. They wanted to try and get me to have twenty scoops of Polycal a day.

I had to see the children's psychiatrist to talk about how I felt about still being in hospital. The psychiatrist phoned the ward when she was ready for me and mum wheeled me over to her office in my wheelchair as I was still too weak to walk.

My mum and I had been waiting for Chris (my brother) to phone us over a job interview that he had been on as he promised to let us know how he had got on.

We were talking to this very stern looking woman (the psychiatrist) over an office desk when both mine and mum's mobiles went off: we only had them on vibrate, but if looks could kill both mum and I would be dead now. The psychiatrist told us both off and TOLD us to turn our phones off while we were talking to her. Mum explained why the phones were on and she told us to take the call and turn off the phones. My brother got the job which made the telling off worth it. Mum and I could not stop laughing. Mum said she felt like a naughty school girl. The psychiatrist said she did not feel the need to see me again as I did not come across as being depressed, but I could have told her that when I went in the room.

Lollipop Radio:
Lollipop is the hospital radio station and because I was interested in radio presenting and before coming into hospital I had my own one hour voluntary radio show on a Saturday morning at Wythenshawe FM,

which I did with one of my friends. It was great fun and we got to play some real cool music as well as doing requests for anyone who would ring us up. Mum wheeled me over to the hospital radio station, which was over in the main hospital in my wheelchair so that I could talk over the air to the children on my ward. While I was there Julie (Haley out of Correnation St') called to see me, and because I was not at my bed one of the nurse brought Julie over to meet me at the radio station and Julie wheeled me back to my ward and told me all her news and what I had been missing on Correnation St". We had a great laugh. We have been talking about ghosts on the ward and some of the nurses I had made friends with told me some funny stories about things that had happened to them when they were working nights. My mum was still sleeping on a chair next to my bed and said she would not walk over the car park late at night, I wonder why?

The weather had been really nice and when my dad came to visit me he asked if I felt like a trip round the hospital grounds, which I did, so he got my wheelchair and took me round the grounds of the hospital, I sat and watched the birds for a while and then dad took me over to the canteen so that he could have a drink. I tried a hot chocolate and managed to drink about half a cup before starting to feel sick. So dad wheeled me back to the ward so that I could lie down for a while.

6th June 2005:
Dr. Dixit called to see me and said he would call back later to talk about my progress during the previous week. Later that afternoon, my mum, Dr Dixit, my nurse, and I went into the parents' room for a private meeting, we talked about how things were going and about me going home (at last), Dr. Dixit mentioned that perhaps I should go home for the day and return to sleep at the hospital. But I so much wanted to go home as I was meant to be attending a charity function with When You Wish upon a Star which was being held that Friday. I mentioned this to Dr. Dixit and told him how important it was to me, so he agreed I could go home on the Thursday for good. Yes..Yes..YES! But, on the understanding he could arrange all the medical care I needed transferred down to my local hospital in time, otherwise I would not be able to go home. I was still very much underweight, which they were not happy about. Mum told them I would eat better at home and they agreed to try this.

Kirsty's Story

9th June 2005:
It was a great feeling when dad arrived on the ward to collect me and once again I was struck by how fortunate I was that I had great parents who took such good care of me. I was so excited, I couldn't wait to be in my own home. I can't believe it, it felt really strange being home and being able to sleep in my own bed for the first time in months.

Can I just say, remember that every person is different, so please if you have Scoliosis or know someone with it, don't assume their experience will be like mine and different hospitals may provide different care! I was in one of the best children's hospital in the Manchester area and received the best care ever. It was just unfortunate that the tumours on my spine caused so many problems.

Scoliosis isn't an illness or disease, it's a Condition or describing word if you want, for curves in the spine. Personally, I think people in schools should be aware of the condition. Apparently, they used to check all children's spines years ago, but strangely have stopped now and so many cases go undetected.

Since being discharged from hospital

29th June 2005:
Things are going ok. I am still attending the hospital weekly but I have started to put some weight on even though I am still in a lot of pain. My Dietician (Cathy) says the Scandishakes, which are high in supplements, protein and calories are helping me and I still have to take Polycal in my food and drinks. I still have a long way go as I lost 2st in weight. But I'll get there.

7th September 2005:
I started back at school today but due to me having to go to hospital every week for physiotherapy I am only in school four days a week and school send transport for me, which is really kind of them. I am getting really tired and fall a sleep when I get home for about an hour.

9th September 2005:
I had to go to Pendlebury Children's Hospital today to see Mr. Oxborrow, I have been in a lot of pain and I am still having bouts of being sick. He thinks that I may have an infection so blood test were done, Mr. Oxborrow also arranges for me to be seen at the children's pain clinic in Sheffield, I am also sent for an x-ray, the x-ray is looking good apart from a slight kink at the bottom of the spine, which Mr. Oxborrow is not too worried about at this point but which will have to be kept an eye on.

Mr. Oxborrow also tells me he wants to talk to Mr. Thorn over the amount of tumours, which are on my spine to see if he can think of anything that can be done.

29th September 2005:
Not a lot of change really. Unfortunately, I am still being sick and today when I was on my way to Sheffield Children's Hospital to see the Pain Management Team the ambulance guy had to pull over because I was

being so ill. I have been put on some new Pain killing tablets (Tramadol) and we will see how they go over the next two weeks.

Tramadol is used to relieve moderate to moderately severe pain. It may be used to treat pain caused by surgery and chronic conditions such as cancer or joint pain and it works by decreasing the body's sense of pain.

Two weeks later and getting side effects from Tramadol:
Unfortunately, Tramadol caused me some side effects, which were dizziness, headache, drowsiness and blurred vision. My sickness was getting worse, and I really did not feel very well and I was advised to stop taking it. Not everyone gets side effects from Tramadol: lots of people get the relief from pain from them.

15th October 2005:
Not a lot of changes over the past month really except up until last week I had continued to gain weight but I have lost some on my last visit and I have got to go back in two weeks to see how things are then. Still having Physio' in the hydro' pool every week.

I received a phone call telling me I have to go back to Sheffield Children's on the 10th November to talk about some other treatment to help with the pain.

10th November 2005:
I went to Sheffield Children's Hospital today to meet with the pain management team. The morning started when mum and I were picked up from home at around 8.45am by Mark who was our ambulance driver for the day.

We got to the hospital about 10.45am and the team was waiting for us. We chatted and spoke about how things had been going. Dr. Goddard decided to try a new tablet (Amitriptyline 10mg). He explained that I would have to build up the dosage due to one of the side effects making you tired and they can also affect the heart rhythm so I had to have an E.C.G, which was over in another hospital. Then it was back in the ambulance where Mark took us over for the E.C.G.

What is an E.C.G?

ECG (electrocardiogram) is a test that measures the electrical activity of the heart. I had about 10 self adhesive electrodes pads attached to selected locations of my skin on my arms, legs and chest. The test was completely painless and took less than five minute to perform once the leads are in position. After the test, the electrodes pads are removed. My consultant will review the paper printout of the E.C.G.

The doctor will phone my mum and let her know if it's safe for me to take these new tablets. They think my pain is going to be difficult to treat due to the tumours on the spine but I will give anything a try to see how it goes.

I have got to go back to Sheffield Children's on the 1st December 2005 to let them know if these new tablets are doing any good.

11th November 2005:

I had to go and see Dr. Bennett this afternoon. She was pleased that I have put on weight and I am to continue with what I am doing. I still have to go to hospital every week for physio' in the hydro' pool. Hydrotherapy involves special exercises, which take place in a warm-water pool (usually at a temperature of 33-37ºC). The warmth of the water and the exercise tend to make me feel tired after treatment but I know it's for my own good and I have still got a long way to go yet.

1st December 2005:

I went to Sheffield Children's Hospital today, Chris (our ambulance driver) picked mum and me up about 7.45am and we got to the hospital around 10.20am. We went to the wrong hospital at first, which was not our fault as we were told to go to the adult hospital.

I had to try some relaxation exercises. Mum tried the relaxation exercises too, which made us both laugh. Well, they do say laughter is the best medicine.

The relaxation exercise's we did were called:

The Laura Mitchell Method of Relaxation:

I am going to be sent a relaxation tape that I can do at home, I have got to try and do the relaxation exercise's twice a day in between doing my physio', which I also still do twice a day. We also spoke about how when you are in pain it can be like being on a rollercoaster, On a good day we may get up and do a lot but then not feel so well and end up having to rest then get up do too much again and having to rest again. It is best to pace your self by balancing rest and activity so that the pain is not exacerbated unduly. I am going to have a go at doing these relaxation exercises and mum said she will do the exercises with me. I have to go back on the 5th January 2006.

14th December 2005:
I went for my physio' to day and my physio' was worried that my legs, hands and tummy were all very swollen so she said she was not going to do any physio' and that I was to go to A&E and let them have a look at me. When the doctor saw me he made sure I did not have any blood clots in my legs and was very puzzled as to why my tummy was so swollen (it looked as though I had a football up my jumper), I felt very unwell too. After chatting it was suggested I may have done too much when I was in Lapland or it could have something to do with the tablets (Amitriptyline). I went home and was told to rest but if got any worse I was come back.

Mum phoned the pain clinic to tell them what had happened and even though they had not heard of this happening before with these tablets it was suggested that I came off them, which I did over a few days.

5th January 2006:
Back to Sheffield Children's Hospital today. We chatted about how the relaxation exercises were going, which are ok at the time of doing them but if I am at school or out and about I cannot do them. My pain doctor also wants me to try Nortriptyline 10mg for the pain; I have to take two tablets at night and one tablet in the morning as an alternative to Amitriptyline. Nortriptyline can be used to treat chronic pain, and headaches. In the meantime I am to continue with weekly physio' at my local hospital.

27th January 2006 Pendlebury Hospital
I went to see Mr. Neil Oxborrow today over the pain in my back. We chatted for a while and I was sent for a full x-ray of the spine,

Mr. Oxborrow was happy with the x-ray but a little concerned over some other issues. He sent me to have a blood test to make sure there

Kirsty Ashton

was no infection in my spine. I asked if I could have the magic cream.... Lol....Waaaaaaa, the real name for this cream is "Emla Cream". The cream was put onto my skin and a soft see through plaster was placed over the top of the cream. It was then left for about 30 minutes. When the time was up, the cream was wiped off the skin. The area now felt "numb" and it did not hurt when I had the needle. I don't like needles. It took four nurses to try and find a vein because my veins tend to riddle or just disappear. Finally the needle is pushed in the hope it works first time, which would be a miracle. It normally takes four or five attempts and an anesthetists being called for to take over the job and even he has problems finding a suitable vein.

Mr. Oxborrow also wanted me to have an urgent MRI Scan of my brain and full spine scan. Mr. Oxborrow said the scan will be done within the next two to three weeks. He also asked me to make an urgent appointment with my GP as I have been bleeding from my bottom.

8th February 2006:
I had to attend Sheffield Children's Hospital today to see Sue, Sue is part of the pain management team. Toby was my ambulance driver for the day and we did not get lost this time. When we arrived we had a quick chat with Sue to bring her up to date with how things have been. Sue asked me if I would like to go in the sensory room, to do my relaxation session. I have never been in a sensory room before, but I have always wanted to see what a sensory room looked liked.

When mum and I walked into this room there was a large blue mat on the floor, a large silver glitter ball hung from the ceiling and soft lighting that changed colour.

Sue wanted to make a tape that I could take home with me and listen to when I am in pain. Sue invited mum to come in the room too, so mum and I both lay on the mat with pillows propped under our heads.

I don't know what it was but as soon as Sue started to talk both mum and I started laughing: we were not being rude, Sue is great, we just got a fit of the giggles. In the end mum went out of the room so Sue could make the tape recording.

Kirsty's Story

I also saw Dr. John Godard, he was not feeling very well and I think he needed to see a doctor him self, I had been getting bad side effects from Nortriptyline too.

So Dr. Godard wanted me to try Gabapentin 300mg for the pain and said he would call me in two weeks to see how I was reacting to them. Gabapentin is a medicine that is mainly used to treat epilepsy. But it can also be used to treat nerve pain. Nerve pain is often not relieved by normal painkillers. I can use the Gabapentin in conjunction with my other painkillers to try and improve my pain relief.

9th February 2006: Time for my M.R.I Scan
I went for my Brain and full Spine MRI Scan today. I took my teddy with me for luck and his nose fell off Waaaaaaaa. My mum is going to try and glue it back on. My mum came in the scan room with me. The scan took about 50 minutes because of me having a brain ("Yes" I have got brain, or so I'm told) and a full spine scan done and as promised I stayed really still whilst the doctor performed the scan. He said I had done really well, managing to stay still for so long, but he never gave me a sticker! I will try and get one when I return. No one cheats Kirsty out of her sticker.

The results will be sent to Mr. Oxborrow and he will phone me next week with the results.

11th February 2006:
The operation to remove the three tumours in my leg has been put back to the 29th March 2006, which is better for me as I am on holiday from school from the 31st March for two weeks. I am still going to the hospital every Wednesday and they say I will have to keep going for a while yet.

20th February 2006:
Hospital phoned to say they now want me in on the 1st March to do the operation on my leg but I have school exams on the 8th March and I am back on antibiotics due to an ear infection, I have had to tell them I will have to keep with the 29th March appointment and I have also got a big event. I am doing for "When You Wish upon a Star" and I am not about to let them down.

I have had news about the spinal mattress I should have one very soon as it was going to be ordered today.

28th February 2006:
I had to go to my doctors again last week over the ear infection, which I still have. My doctor gave me a letter to take to the hospital. On arrival at the hospital the doctor decided to vacuum my ear to try and clear the discharge. He then told me that my eardrum was perforated. A perforated eardrum is a hole or rupture in the eardrum, a thin membrane that separates the ear canal and the middle ear.

I have got to see an ENT specialist and have a hearing test in May to assess any loss of hearing.

I now have my spinal mattress at last: it's a little too early to say how things are just yet as I have only slept on it twice.

22nd March 2006:
Back from the hospital after having my pre' operation check to make sure I am ok for surgery on my leg next Wednesday (29th March 2006). I was meant to be going into hospital on the Wednesday morning but they have decided to bring me in the day before as I am first on the list and at the moment I have still got this ear infection and they want to see how my temperature goes, I may also need to have an ultrasound scan done on my leg and some blood tests before surgery. Not sure how long I will be in but not very long I hope.

1st April 2006:
I am home from hospital after a couple of days stay, which is not too bad. I had three tumours removed from inside my leg in various places, I have got to go back to hospital on Wednesday (5th April 2006, my birthday waaaaa) to have the stitches removed. I stayed on the Starlight Ward and my mum stayed with me. We had our own room, which had its own shower and toilet and everyone was really kind.

Kirsty's Story

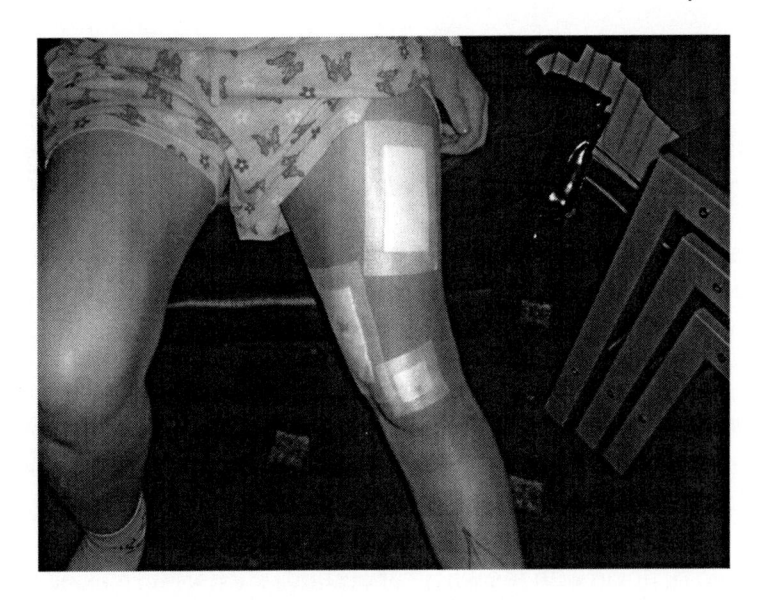

The operation took two and half-hours. My leg is very painful at the moment and very heavily bandaged, I have been told not to do very much for the next three weeks. I will get the results when I next see the doctor in six weeks.

12th April 2006:
I went to see Mr. Thorn yesterday; he wanted to talk over the spinal scan I had done a few weeks ago. Mr. Thorn told me that the scan showed that I have at least one tumour on every nerve on and around my spine and he is not surprised that I am in a lot of pain.

Mr. Thorn mentioned that some of the tumours look like NF2 tumours and he thinks I may have NF2 and NF1 but. Mum mentioned to him that this was said last year too and none of the doctors could really agree and that they were meant to be doing some test to make sure one way or the other, which was never done,

Mr. Thorn said he could only go off what he could see on the scan.

I will have the spinal scan done again in 12 months unless the pain gets any worse as some of the tumours have grown and this is what is causing all the pain in my groin and the tingling in my fingers. He said they could try doing an operation now but the risk of paralysis was high. So I don't want to take the risk.

In the meantime I have to continue attending hospital weekly for physio' until I am a little stronger.

7th May 2006:
I am attending the hospital everyday this week.

I have been told that it may be a good idea if I went back into my back brace to help support my spine and that that this may help with the pain. I go for the fitting for my new back brace next Friday.

I do physio' for at least 30 minutes twice a day as well as attending hospital weekly for physio' (hydro'). My family helps me with my physio' each morning and night. I also do relaxation exercises twice a day where I lie down and listen to a tape recording lasting about 30 minutes each time. Before I start my relaxation exercise, I put on comfortable clothing and then lie down with the whole of my body supported, making myself totally comfortable and closing my eyes. The tape recording is tailored for me and is about me going on a journey and swimming with dolphins. This is very relaxing at the time.

I am managing to sleep better with the spinal mattress, I still have problems getting settled but I am not waking up as much in the night now.

10th May 2006:
I was at Sheffield Children's Hospital today. The appointment went well and I did some more relaxation exercises with Sue.

I mentioned to Sue that I keep getting swollen ankles; she said I have some fluid retention (medically known as oedema) more so in one leg than the other and that I should mention it to my doctor so that it can be investigated more.

Oedema is a build-up of excess fluid in the body tissues. If the fluid is in the tissue under the skin it leads to a puffy, shiny appearance and a doughy feel. Most commonly, oedema is seen in the ankles or legs, as the fluid is gravity-dependent.

Sue suggested that mum massages my back, shoulders and legs; this may also help reduce the swelling in the ankles. My next appointment is in July.

11th May 2006:
I went for the results on the tumours that I had removed from my leg and the good news is they were ok and nothing nasty. The scars are healing nicely and I have just got to keep putting the cream on for about three months. I don't need to go back unless I have any further problems.

12th May 2006:
I had to see my E.N.T doctor today, I knew my ear was still infected as not only was I in pain with them but I had to see my GP yesterday and he put me on some different eardrops and antibiotics in the hope it would clear up the infection.

The ENT doctor had to vacuum both ears out before I could have a hearing test done, which I passed and my hearing was fine. He thinks I may have eczema in my ears. Eczema is a common skin condition that can cause mild to extreme irritation. When eczema is mild, it often causes dry, hot and itching skin. Eczema causes raw, broken and cracked skin. Scratching the irritated skin can result in oozing or weeping patches, which are prone to infection. The condition is not contagious and may flare up at anytime.

I have got to go back in six months, but before if the ears start weeping again so that they can be vacuumed out.

I have to go back in the back brace and go for a fitting on the 19th May. It's not so bad though, I only have to wear it when I'm in a lot of pain and the tablets have not helped. I have also got my exams over the next few weeks so lots of study will be necessary.

19th May 2006:
Today I went for the fitting for my new back brace, as you will see from the pictures. To make the mould for the brace I was wrapped in plaster of Paris bandages. When this dried (only a few minutes) the mould was cut away from me. This procedure is messy but does not hurt. I was given a choice of colour and I was going for a really bright colour but then decided to stick with white. The brace will be made from a solid plastic going all the way up my back and will be fastened from the front with soft straps. I will also need to wear a soft cotton vest/top underneath the brace, to stop the brace rubbing my skin and keep me

comfortable. I have been getting a lot of pain, especially in my legs, back and groin and it's hoped the brace may help with the pain.

The brace will be ready on the 2nd June 2006.

Most children with scoliosis have mild curves — less than 20 degrees and probably won't need a brace or surgery. Periodic checkups are needed; to be sure the curve doesn't progress. Children who are still growing need checkups every three to six months to see if there have been any changes in the curvature of their spine. Wearing a brace won't cure scoliosis, or even improve the curve, but it usually prevents further progression of the curve.

A brace will not be effective unless I wear it as prescribed. The brace does feel uncomfortable and awkward at times. But after a couple of weeks, however, wearing a brace begins to feel normal again.

2nd June 2006:
Went to Pendlebury Children's Hospital for my new back brace today but unfortunately there were some problems with it when Claire tried it on me (not touching where it should) so Claire is sending it back to have some remolding work done. I now get the brace on the 23rd June 2006.

9th June 2006:
I have been out of hospital one year today and it feels great even if I am still going to hospital every week. It's wonderful to be home.

I went for a dry land physio' today. My new physio' is called Mark and after doing my physio' he decided it would be a good idea if I was to see an Occupational Therapist.

What do Occupational therapists do?
Occupational therapists work with people who have a physical disability; they help people who have difficulties with practical, everyday tasks. The aim of occupational therapy is to enable you to live as independently as possible – at home, or in employment and give advice on disability equipment. They are going to give me some equipment to help me put my socks and shoes on and just look at things that will help me be more independent really.

Mark also found a problem with my foot (I have fallen a few times) and he wants me to be measured for a Foot brace as he thinks I may have foot drop due to me not being able to lift my foot up fully, which is the reason I keep falling.

23rd June 2006:
I received my new back brace today and it was just as well as. Mum and I decided we would go shopping for some new clothes for our holidays. Unfortunately on the way, the bus, which we were travelling on, was involved in an accident. The bus driver braked hard and we were slung forward with some force resulting in mum hitting her head, shoulder and injuring her neck and top of her spine. I suffered injury to my neck and spine too. Both mum and I were in so much pain we had to go to the hospital A/E department where the nurse looked us both over and told mum she had lots of inflammation around the top of her back. We were given pain killing tablets. The next thing I remember was we were both immediately taken into "resus" and made to lie flat on a bed and the doctor put us both into a neck brace.

We had to stay like this until x-rays were taken. We had both suffered whiplash and mum had a badly bruised shoulder too and given tablets to help take the inflammation down at the top of her back.

Whiplash occurs when the soft tissue in the spine is stretched and strained after the body is thrown in a sudden, forceful jerk, which is what happened on the bus. Both mum an I were discharged after x-rays were taken.

When we got home we wrapped a bag of frozen peas in a towel to see if this would help to take the inflammation down. We were only comfortable lying on the bed with our heads resting on the ice bag; we did this for about 20 minutes with our heads also supported by a pillow. The pain was really bad.

We are due to go on holiday on the 1st July to Florida and at the moment are finding it really difficult to sit for any length of time.

20th July 2006:
We had a wonderful holiday in Florida but it was ruined by mum and I not being able to sit in the car for very long due to the pain we were both in from the whiplash we had suffered.

I am undergoing tests at the moment to see if I have both NF1 and NF2. The blood test will take three months but I had my brain scan yesterday. The doctor had problems getting the needle in my veins but managed in the end. I should receive the results in the next week a so.

27th July 2006:
Went to Sheffield Children's to see Susanne Davis. We chatted for about three hours and I was given a V.Tens Plus to use for the pain and my Gabapentin was increased. I have been asked not to use the T.E.N's until I have spoken with Mr. Oxborrow tomorrow to make sure it will be safe to put near the tumours on my spine.

How T.E.N's work
Small pads are placed on or near the area of your pain and when the TEN's unit is turned on you feel a soothing pulse that is sent via the pads through the skin and along your nerve fibres. And the level of the pulses is controlled by you the user at all times, which hopefully will suppress the pain signals to the brain. T.E.N's also encourages the body to produce higher levels of its own natural pain killing chemicals called Endorphins and Encephalins.

Only use a TEN's on medical advice as they are not suitable for everyone.

28th July 2006:
Went to Pendlebury Children's Hospital today for a check-up on my spine. I saw Mr. Oxborrow who sent me for an x-ray. I mentioned that I had been in a lot of pain with my back and unfortunately Mr. Oxborrow told me that my back had gone worse and that some new tumours had also grown on the spine. He mentioned further surgery in which he would place rods all the way to the top of my spine but I am not keen for him to do this at the moment as there are too many risk involved and at the end of the day he was not sure himself if it would make any difference at this stage. He wants me to have a bone scan and he

Kirsty's Story

is going to have a chat with the neurosurgeon to see what steps they should take next.

I asked Mr. Oxborrow about the T.E.N's and he was unsure if it would be safe for me to use so I have now got to talk with Mr. Thorn who is the neurosurgeon.

7th August 2006:
I am still waiting to hear back from Mr. Thorn to see if it is safe to use the V T,E,N's Plus. I have been in a lot of pain so the sooner I can start using it the better.

24th August 2006:
I am still having problems with my ears, which as been going on since last year. I have been going every week to see the E.N.T doctor who cleans my ears of the pus so that eardrops can get to the infection. Stuart (my E.N.T doctor) is really nice and said he is not letting me go until he knows this ear infection has gone this time.

If you have your Ears cleaned out at the hospital:
Before starting treatment with eardrops, you'll probably have your ear cleaned out by a specialist doctor. The cleaning will get rid of the bits of skin and pus that was blocking your ears so that the eardrops can get through to the infection.

The main symptoms of an ear infection with discharge are:

- Pus coming out of your ear

- Not hearing as well as you used to

- Ear pain or discomfort.

You may get symptoms in one or both of your ears. You might have non-stop ear discharge, or your symptoms may come and go.

When your doctor examines your ear, he or she will shine a light into your ear and look down an instrument called an otoscope. This is to see whether your eardrum has a hole in it. Some doctors use a microscope to take a better look.

Your doctor will also ask you questions about your symptoms and how long they have been going on. This will help him or her to work out whether you have a long-term (chronic) infection or a short-term (acute) infection.

1st September 2006: Brain Scan Results

Mum got a call from the doctor at Pendlebury Children's Hospital to day to say the results of the brain scan were good and nothing to worry about, which was great news and he also told my mum that it was safe for me to use the V Plus T.E.N's machine.

NF2 Blood Test

You may remember I mentioned that my doctors at Pendlebury Children's Hospital were concerned that I may have both NF1 and NF2 (very rare if I do have both) due to how some of the tumours look and the nerves they have grown on. Well the blood test I had for this went wrong so unfortunately I have got to have it done again on Monday and will now have to wait until December before I get the results as it takes three months for this test result to come back.

I am still going to see Stuart (one of the E.N.T Doctors) every week and I have had a few ear swabs done. Things are still no better with regards the ear infection so Stuart wants me to see this other doctor next week. My ears are really bad at the moment so I'm not sure what will happen.

Marc my physio' measured me for my foot brace today and that should be with me in the next week. I am not sure what it is like yet only that part of it will go under my foot and in my shoe and the other part will go up my leg with Velcro straps around the leg. Drop foot is not a disease but a symptom of an underlying problem. Depending on the cause, foot drop may be temporary or permanent. When I last saw my spine specialist he mentioned that the cause of my foot drop would be due to the tumours pressing on my spine and he was going to talk to Mr. Thorn over this new problem.

27th September 2006:
I have been going back and to, to the hospital with this ear infection that has still not cleared up. I have now been told I have a perforated eardrum at what the doctor said that it was at the seven o'clock point. A perforated eardrum would normally heal by itself, although sometimes surgery is required. The doctor wants to see me again in a few months and if the ear is still perforated, an operation to repair the eardrum called a myringoplasty will be performed.

If you have a perforated eardrum, you may get the following symptoms in the affected ear:

- Earache, or discomfort,
- Discharge of liquid or pus from your ear,

A perforation or rupture in the eardrum (in other words a hole in the thin layer of tissue which separates the external ear canal from the middle ear).

Physio'
I am still having physio' in the hydro' pool weekly and when I went today, Marc my physio' said that he was going to contact Pendlebury over the foot brace as the brace that I have been sent is not working and I need to be fitted for a different kind.

Mum also received a call over the bone scan to tell her that I should be having it done in the next couple of weeks. The pain in my back has been really bad recently and I keep falling on the floor my legs are really bruised from falling.

6th October 2006:
Health wise, things are still very much the same. The pain in the back is a little worse and I find my self getting very tired.

11th October 2006:
I have been getting very breathless recently so mum took me to see our family G.P today who sent me for an urgent chest X-ray.

A chest x-ray allows a look at the inside of the chest. Rays that pass through the body to create a black and white negative type picture achieve this. A chest x-ray examination itself is a painless procedure and I was only in the X-ray department for about 10 minutes

18th October 2006: Time for X-ray results:
My doctor told me that the chest it self looked clear but the radiologist had mentioned that he could see a tumour coming out of the right side of my lung so I have got to go and see a chest specialist next week for more tests.

I have also got to have an ultrasound scan of my kidneys as I have been getting a lot of pain in my back, ribs and sides (I have had a kidney infection). This is to make sure that I don't have any tumours on the kidney.

27th October 2006: Spent the day at Pendlebury Children's Hospital
My morning started by mum and me being picked up by one of my ambulance guys (Mike).

When I arrived at the hospital I went over to Gamma Camera Unit to have some EMLA Cream (magic cream) applied. This cream numbs the area to be injected to stop it from hurting me. I had to return to the department an hour later to have the injection.

My next stop was to see Clair who is making my new back brace and foot brace.

Just time to go and have a drink before I head back to the Gamma Unit. I was given an injection, which contained 550 MBq radioactivity into a vein in my arm. I had to return to the Department 2 hours later for the scan. With two hours to kill, I decided to visit the nurses who looked after me when I was very poorly last year. Mum and I also went and had some dinner.

Having my back and foot braces made

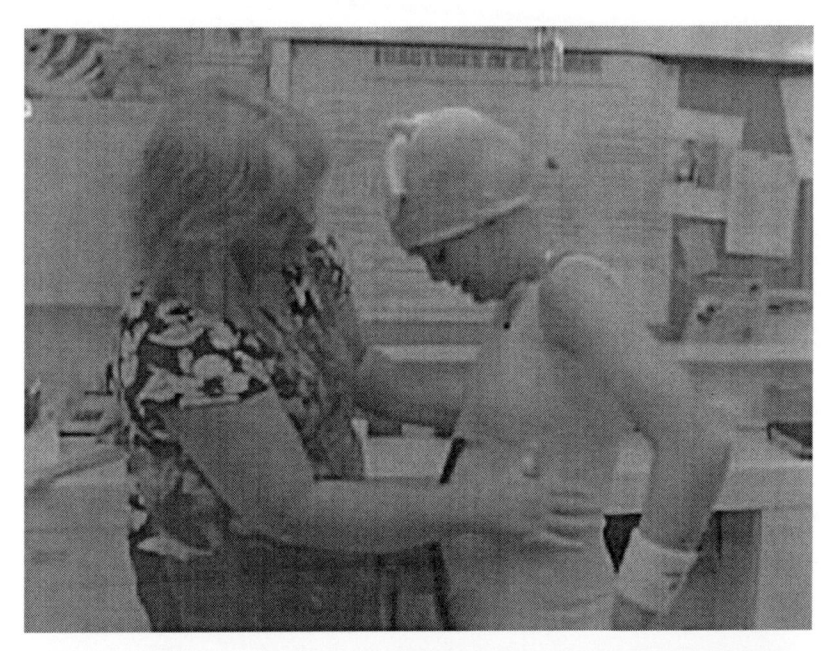

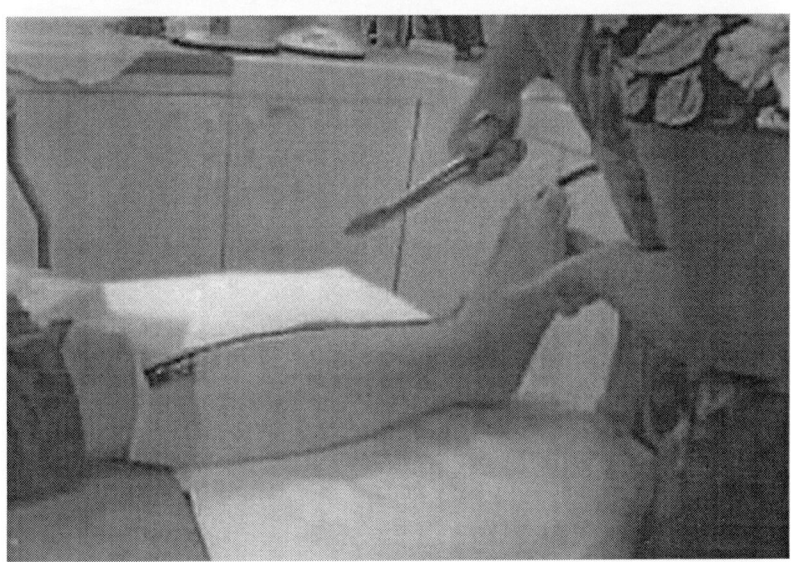

Trying to keep still while the scan is being done.

Back to the Gamma Unit for scan

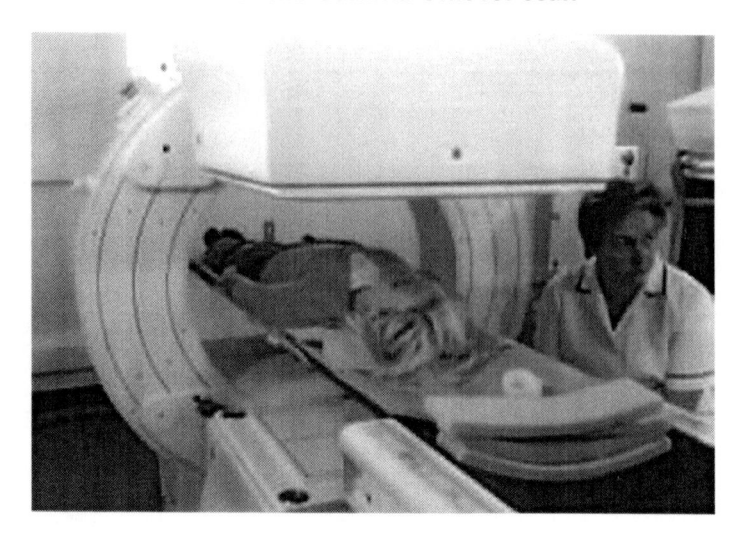

Going inside the scan.

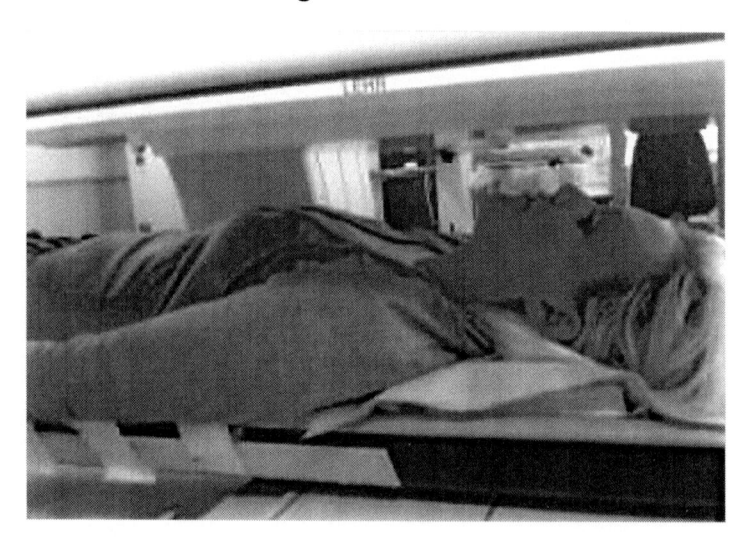

What is a Bone Scan?

A bone scan is a very sensitive technique and when the radioactive substance is injected, it travels through the bloodstream and collects in your bones. The purpose of this study is to take pictures of my bones to help the doctor diagnose how my condition is affecting me.

After emptying my bladder, I was asked to lie down on a couch, and pictures of my bones were taken using a gamma camera. I did not need to take off any clothing, only remove my jewellery. In order to get good pictures, the camera was very close to me and I had to remain very still. The scan took about 30-45 minutes. My result will be sent to the doctor who requested the study.

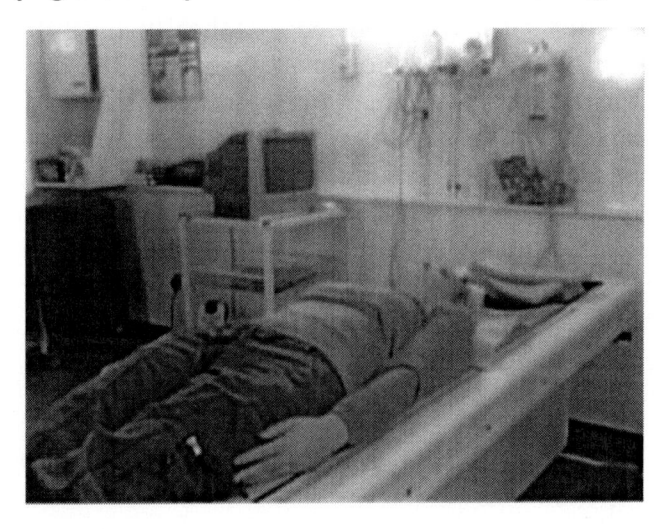

Trying to lie very still while the bone scan is being done.

1st November 2006:

I have had a busy few weeks and lots of hospital visits. I went to see the doctor over the tumour on the lung. He was going to keep me in hospital because he was worried that I may have a blood clot but decided I could go home on the condition that I came back the next day. Urgent blood tests were done along with other tests.

Back at the hospital the following day and I was told the test results were inconclusive and that the blood test came back slightly raised and that my breathing was very fast. He was unsure if I should be kept in or not, I was at the hospital over four hours before he decided I could go home only to return the following day for a VQ scan (ventilation perfusion scan). This is a type of radionucleid scan which uses various radio-isotopes (substances which emit radiation) to assess the blood supply to the lungs and how well each part of the lung is ventilated. I had the VQ scan to check that I did not have any clots on the lung (pulmonary embolism).

Technique and preparation:
No specific preparation was required. This test took about 15-20 minutes and was done as an outpatient. When I arrived in the department for the VQ scan it was in the Nuclear Medicine Department, which was situated in the X-ray department. I was asked to lie on a couch and a small needle was inserted into my vein. I then had a small injection of a radioactive substance. The radiographer then positioned the camera next to my chest and told me to keep still. The radiographer stayed in the room as did my mum and he watched the images as they were displayed on a television monitor. Six or eight different views were taken, each one taking a few minutes. I also had to breathe in a radioactive gas through a mask, which was a little uncomfortable. The process only took about 15 minutes. The two sets of images are then compared. The only discomfort I experienced was that of the injection and the mask. The radiologist said he would write a report and send it to my doctor who asked for the scan to be done.

11th November 2006:
I was in so much pain this evening that dad took me to the A & E department. Mum was out but when Dad sent a text to Mum to say he was taking me to the hospital as I was not so well. Mum said she would meet us at the hospital. In the hospital, blood and urine test were done and again my breathing was very fast. But the doctor thinks the pain is down to the tumours round my kidney area. I was allowed home later that evening and told to rest and come back if things got any worse.

Kirsty's Story

Results Back
The doctor phoned to say he was happy with the VQ scan (no clots were found in the lungs). But that he now wants me to have some lung function test done with my breathing being so fast and my lungs being so small.

14th November 2006:
I received my new foot and back brace today.

15th November 2006
I had to go and see my doctor to day, I received a letter saying she wanted to see me over some test results. The scan on my kidney was good and there was no tumours in or on the kidney but it did show that I had tumours on the tissues and muscles around them so I have got to go and see this other doctor now, which should be before Christmas. I have also been losing weight and have lost about 6lb over 4 weeks, but don't know why.

Charity Ball
I have got my big charity Ball on Saturday, which I am really looking forward to.

24th November 2006:
I went to see my doctor yesterday as I have not been feeling very well and I have more and more tumours growing by the day. My doctor felt the ones in my chest area and said she was going to make an urgent appointment with the hospital doctor to see me. I also feel really tired at the moment. But I hope to go to the cinema with Mum tomorrow as I have got the day off college and mum wants to do some Christmas shopping.

4th December 2006:
I am still waiting to hear if the documentary will be going ahead, I will not know until the New Year now. They want to talk to my hospital doctors now and hope to do that in the New Year. Mr. N Oxborrow phoned me yesterday and I explained to him what the film crew hoped to do and he said he was happy to help.

Kirsty Ashton

News on the NF2 Blood test:
You may remember I mentioned that some of my doctors thought that I may have both NF1 and NF2. Well, I am pleased to say that mum received a phone call this week from the hospital to say the blood test results were back and I don't have NF2 only the NF1, which was great news.

I have now seen the hospital doctor
Today I saw the hospital doctor over the pain in my tummy and about the new tumours that have grown around my kidney area. He wants me to have a colonoscopy in the New Year. This is due to some bleeding that I have been having.

What is a colonoscopy?
A colonoscopy is a test where the doctor looks into your large intestine or large bowel.

A colonoscopy is a thin, flexible, telescope. It is about as thick as a little finger. It is passed through the anus and into the colon. It can be pushed all the way round the colon as far as the caecum (where the small and large intestine meet).

The colonoscopy contains fibre optic channels which allows light to shine down so the doctor can see inside your colon.

My doctor advised that I have this test due to the symptoms I was getting such as bleeding from my bottom and pains in the lower abdomen.

My colon needs to be empty so that the doctor can get a clear view. I have to take a special diet for a few days before the test and I have been given some laxatives to take the day before the test. They are going to give me a sedative with being so young. Don't think I would like to be a wake for this test.

9th January 2007: Lung Function Test
I went for The Lung function tests today, which are being done to help determine the cause of my shortness of breath, which I have been getting for a few months now. Lung (or pulmonary) function tests test show how efficiently I am breathing. I was asked to put on a nose-clip so that all my breathing takes place through my mouth, then I had to

breathe into a mouthpiece attached to a machine that measures the air that I breathe in and out.

I had to breathe in a special mix of oxygen and carbon dioxide to see how well my lungs are absorbing the oxygen and excreting the carbon dioxide. I had to take deep breaths then exhale as fully as possible, I had to keep repeating the test over and over again as they were not happy with the reading. I think the lady doing the test thought I was not trying hard enough, but I was and it was just making me more and more breathless.

I had a few different breathing exercises to do, which did make me feel dizzy and breathless.

I had to stay and see the doctor for the results of the test.
The doctor said that he was not sure what was going on as the lung function test came back with some abnormalities but he was still not sure if it was anything to do with the tumour on the lung or not. He thought the tumour was on the outside of my lung when he first looked at the chest x-rays but after having the Gamma scan he said the tumour was inside the lung and that he would keep an eye on it. He is now going to have a chat with another Chest Specialist to discuss the test results and to see what he should do next. He will phone and let me know.

11th January 2007: Sheffield Children's Hospital.
I went to Sheffield Children's hospital today to see Dr. Godard, Sue and Rebecca who are all part of the pain team.

After having a chat with Dr. Goddard and the team about how my pain had been Dr. Goddard decided that I should also take Ketamine to help with the pain, I only have to take this when the pain is bad and no more than twice a day.

Ketamine is a powerful anaesthetic drug; Ketamine also works as a pain killing drug. If things don't get any better I may have to think about going on some much stronger medication. Susan also gave me some more advice about the V T.E.N's machine that they gave me last time. I have to go back next Thursday to do some more relaxation exercises with Rebecca.

Kirsty Ashton

I have also seen my E.N.T doctor again this week and unfortunately, I still have the ear infection and I am using antibiotics and ear drops to try and clear this up and I go back next week.

21st January 2007:
I had a few hospital appointments again last week, paying visits to Sheffield Children's, St' Mary's and Wythenshawe Hospital.

At Sheffield I saw Susan who is part of the pain management team and physiotherapist. Mum and I both took part in some relaxation exercises, which was really good after the bad journey we had getting to the hospital. The weather was so bad, we got stuck on the moors and could not ring any body as we could not get a signal on any of our phones. The ambulance guy (Keith) was saying we may have to go back as the weather was getting so bad. We did arrive about 45 minutes late. Susan did the Laura Mitchell Relaxation Exercise and gave me a tape to bring home with it all on. She is also trying to change my spinal mattress for me. I was in so much pain coming home that Keith stopped the ambulance and put me on the stretcher in the ambulance for the rest of the journey home. We got home at 7.15pm feeling really tired, as we set off at 8.30am

St' Mary's Hospital:
I saw both Dr. Sue Huson and Rosemary Abbot. After telling Dr. Huson what had been happening she felt it would be a good idea if I had a PET Scan.

PET stands for Positron Emission Tomography. This is a fairly new type of scan developed in the 1970s. It can show how body tissues are working, as well as what they look like. The scan produces three-dimensional, colour images of the body using radiation.

It can be used to diagnose a health condition, or find out more about how a condition is developing. It can also be used to measure how well treatment for a condition is working.

A PET scan works by detecting radiation inside the body, and makes images that show how the radiation is being broken down. Radiation is given to the body safely as a medicine called a radiotracer, so it goes to the part of your body that needs to be examined. The level of radiation is very small, so it doesn't damage the body.

Dr. Huson is also writing to the plastic surgeon, Mrs. Brains about having the tumours removed from my neck and breast as not only are they both new tumours but they are growing and painful.

24th January 2007:
Tomorrow I'm having the colonoscopy test, I will be admitted to hospital as a day case as I am being sedated to keep me comfortable and to help me relax during the examination. Mum is going to stay with me and the ambulance guys said they will make her lots of brews while she is waiting around.

Colonoscopy Test
Mark, one of my ambulance guys picked Mum and me up this afternoon to take me into hospital for my colonoscopy test.

When I arrived at the hospital, the nurse gave me a gown to change into and spoke to me about the sedation that I was about to have. A Colonoscopy is nearly always done with sedation and painkillers because it would be uncomfortable without.

Because of the problems I have with needles the nurse put some magic cream on my arm in two spots, this was meant to stop the needle from hurting. After two doctors having four attempts each at trying to get the cannula in my arm they had to send for the theatre doctor to have a go. My arms were so bruised, I was crying with the pain (not like me to cry). The nurse was almost crying just watching what I was going through and so was Mum. The doctor said my veins were so bad they just kept blowing every time they went in with the needle. The theatre doctor said the only place left to go now was in the wrist. On his first attempt the vein went again. Mr. Crompton came in to see if he could help and kept saying he was sorry that I was having such a bad time. The only place left now was my other wrist, and at last the doctor managed to get the cannula in. Now both my arms were black from the amount of needles I had (ten in all). Mum gave me a kiss and said she was going to the shop in the hospital to buy me a soft toy to add to my collection for when I came round.

What happened during my colonoscopy?
The sedative made me feel a little drowsy but did not 'put me to sleep'. It is not a general anaesthetic.

I had to lie on my side on a couch. The doctor (Mr. Crompton) gently pushed the end of the colonoscope into my anus and up into my colon. The doctor could then look down the colonoscope and inspect the lining of my colon. This was then transmitted through a camera attachment onto a TV monitor for the doctor to look at. Air was then passed down a channel in the colonoscope into the colon to make the inside lining easier to see. At the end of the procedure the colonoscope was gently pulled out. The colonoscopy took about 30-40 minutes. The doctor said he would send a report but looking at the results everything looked ok, which was great news.

Jason, one of my cool ambulance guys stayed late to bring me home and make sure I was ok "Thanks Jason".

My arms are really painful and black and blue from the doctors trying to get the needles in. Mum bought me a dog (not a real one), which is really cute.

Why I had my colonoscopy?
I was advised to have a colonoscopy due to the symptoms of bleeding from the anus and pains in the lower abdomen that I was getting.

Pendlebury Children's Hospital: Mr. N Oxborrow

26th January 2007:
I saw my favourite doctor today, Mr. N Oxborrow and while I was waiting I saw my favourite nurse (Lesley). She is really cool and very funny. I took some pictures of Lesley on my mobile. I told Lesley I would be putting her picture up on my web site for everyone to see, I don't think she believed me, but I did.

Mr. Oxborrow sent me for an x-ray. When I got back I went in to see him. He looked at the x-rays and was really pleased that my spine had not gone any worse at the top and said the spine had fused well and just looked like a solid piece of bone now. If things stay the same I will not need another operation on my spine.

Kirsty's Story

He then asked why I was using the crutch, I told him about the foot drop and he asked me to take my shoe and foot brace off so that he could have a look. He did a few tests and said "Yes, you do have foot drop" and wanted to know how long it had been like that. He than called another doctor and asked him to arrange for an urgent scan of the bottom of my spine and pelvis area to be done. He was worried that I might have a tumour at the bottom of my spine below the metal work that he did.

My foot drop was very sudden really and this would explain why I had been getting so much pain in my lower back and groin area too. He asked when my next appointment visit for Mr. Thorn would be, which is in April and mentioned that he had spoken to Mr. Thorn about the pain that I was in, Mr. Thorn had told him that I have multiple tumours all over my spine and he was not sure what to do or if removing any of them would help. I have got to go back and see Mr. Oxborrow in six weeks for the results.

2nd February 2007:
My scan went well and was done by Ken. I have known Ken for a long time. He is a really nice guy. Ken said it would take about a week to get my results sent to the doctor but I'm not going back to see Mr. Oxborrow until March.

2nd March 2007:
Dr. Huson has been away and will be writing to the plastic surgeon Mrs. Brains about having the tumours removed from my neck, tummy and breast as not only are they new tumours but they are growing and painful. She will also arrange for me to have the PET Scan done very soon too.

The pain in my back has been really bad and I have not been getting to sleep until after 2am, I have been taking more of the Ketamine, which helps but makes me feel dizzy and a bit funny.

I am also waiting to hear about getting a spenco mattress and electric bed, which doctors think may help me.

Still going to the hospital weekly and Ruth my physio' is really good. We have some fun in the pool, which you may get to see in my TV documentary.

22nd March 2007:
Hospital is still the same. The tumour in my neck has grown since January so I have now got to see this other doctor.

I filmed the short documentary for Well Child, I had a camera follow me around for two days. The documentary was called, "The day in the life of Kay" and was on the community channel in May and June 2007.

After the crew had gone home on the Wednesday we were all really tired, I was going to go to bed but as I was not feeling so well Mum asked me to stay down so that she could keep an eye on me. I am so glad I did because about an hour later we heard this funny sound coming from upstairs that sounded like air in the pipes, Waaaaaa,

When Dad and I went to investigate, we saw the boiler in my room had burst letting out boiling hot water all over my bed, down the wall and on to the carpet. Chris (my brother) managed to get the water shut off and got this guy he knows to come out and have a look at it. He said I was lucky that I was not in the room at the time because the boiler had been giving out toxic fumes, which could have killed me in my sleep.

My bedroom was gutted and we had to get a new boiler, Dad and Mum had the boiler moved into the loft for safety reasons. I was really upset as my teddies were ruined. The story of the boiler bursting made the Sunday paper (The Sunday Post). My bedroom was gutted. I lost four of my teddies, which I was more upset about than anything else.

26th March 2007: Results of M.R.I Scan:
I went for the results of my scan last Friday. The news was not good, and my doctor told me that I had a new cluster of tumours at the bottom of my spine, which had caused the foot to drop. He said one of the tumours was over 3cm and the cut off point was 2 ½ cm. He was also worried that the tumour in my neck had grown yet again and the one in my lung was giving him some worry. He phoned this other doctor on her mobile to tell her about the results and she wanted to see me

Kirsty's Story

the following week when she would be back in the hospital. In the meantime she wanted all my scan reports for her to look at.

My spinal doctor (Mr. N Oxborrow) is really cool and a really nice guy. He asked how old I was and when I told him 16, I thought he was going to say that it was time I went over to the adult hospital. But he said he would not do that to me and that he would continue seeing me at the children's hospital until I was 20 years as an out patient, but if I needed more surgery that would have to be done at a different hospital.

2nd April 2007:
I received a letter from Dr. S Huson this morning telling me that she has written to a Dr. Hules regarding the PET Scan. PET scanning has been shown to be very useful for people with NF1, to show whether any of the neurofibromas has the potential to turn nasty. Dr. Huson said she is not worried about any of my neurofibromas at the moment after examining me in clinic a few weeks ago.

Well, it is my birthday on Thursday, 5th April and I hope to have a brilliant time as I have been in hospital for the last couple of birthdays. I know Mum and I are going out but Mum is not giving much away, lol,

X-rays of my spine before surgery and again after surgery with the rods in:

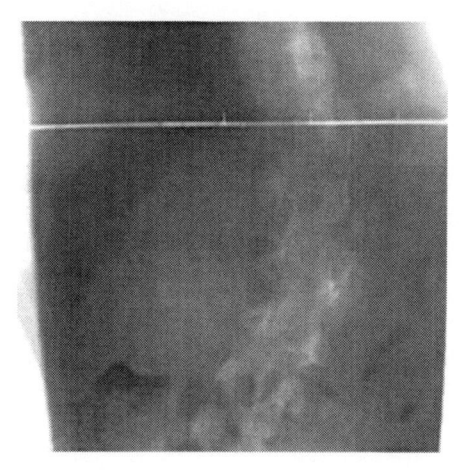

If you look carefully you can see the curve in my spine

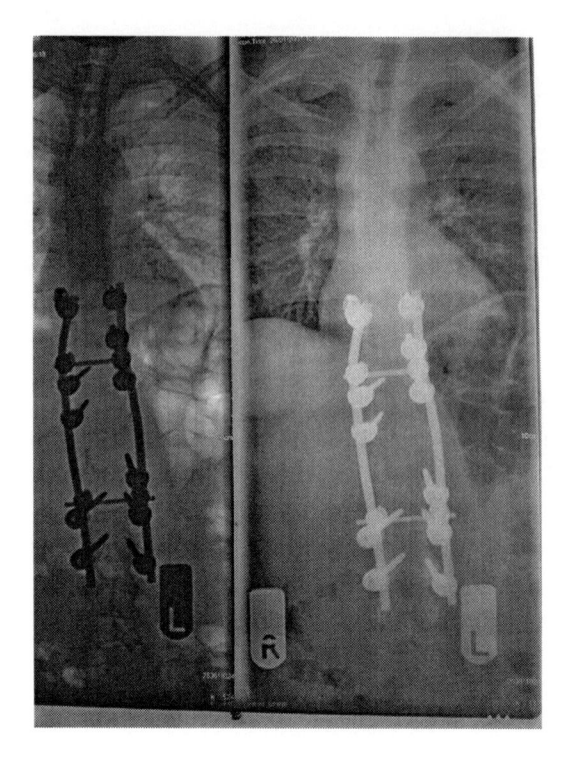

X-Ray showing the rod

5th April 2007:
Well, it's my birthday today and it's great not to spend it in the hospital.

I received a letter about the PET scan this morning along with lots of birthday cards, I go for my scan next week.

10th April 2007:
Mum phoned to confirm my appointment for the PET scan only to be told it had been cancelled Dr. Brennan is going to see me as soon as she has reviewed all the scans etc. Dr. Huson and Dr. Brennan feel that to do the PET scan before then may complicate things further. The Doctors involved in my care need to liaise (Mr. Oxborrow, Mr. Thorne, Dr Barber, Dr. Brennan and Dr. Huson).

Dr Brennan is going to coordinate this. Mum is a little upset by it all as I have been getting a lot of pain in my chest and getting very breathless.

Kirsty's Story

19th April 2007:

Unfortunately the hospital did not go so well today, Mr. Thorn, my neuro' doctor put the scans of my spine up for me to see and told me that I have at least one tumour on every nerve that is coming out of my spine some of which are above 4cm in size. He also thinks that I may be starting with foot drop in my other foot and will need to wear a foot brace on that leg soon. Mum asked him about trying to remove some of the tumours and he said that it would cause more damage if he did and he was not sure if he could remove any. I took pictures of some of the scans.

(Sorry if I upset anyone by these scan pictures).

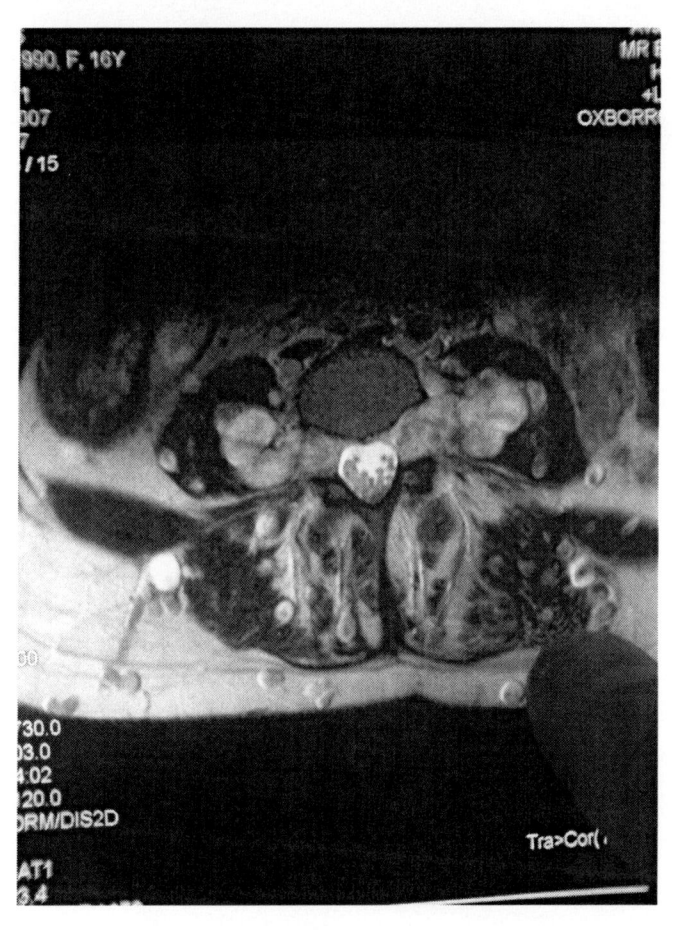

The doctor points to the tumours

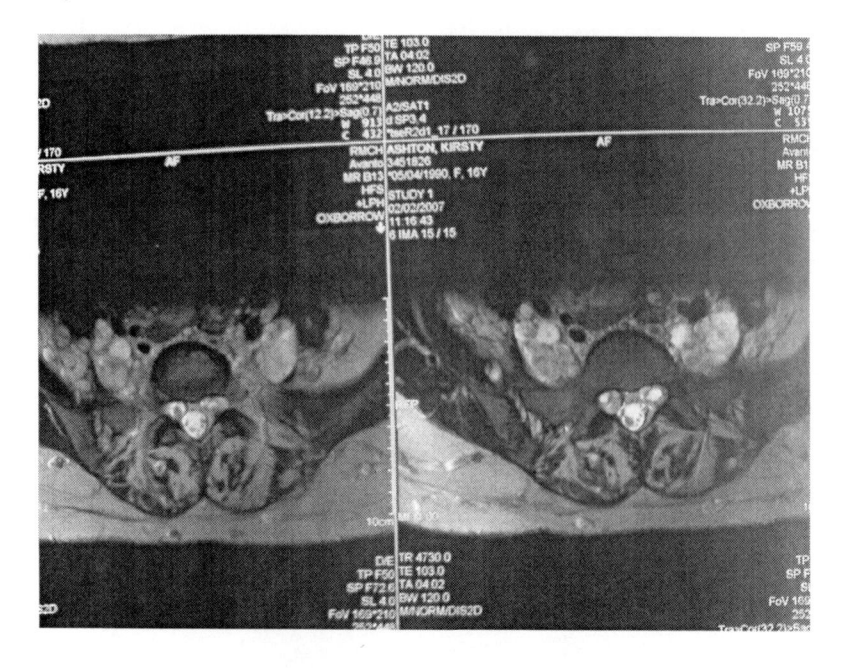

Scan looking down the spine

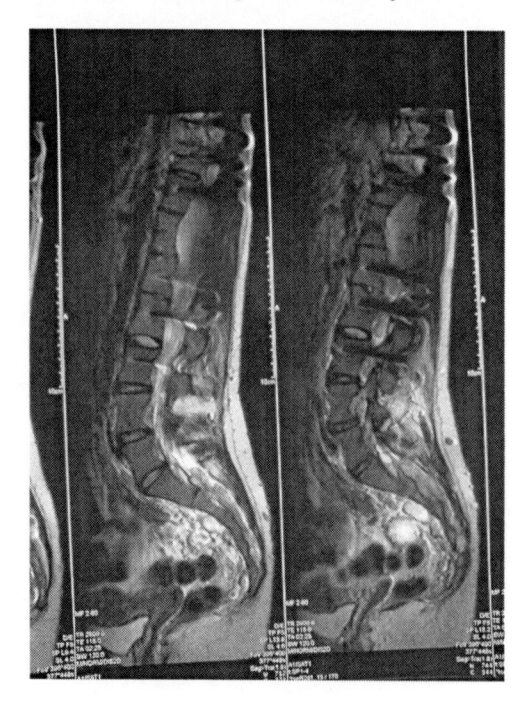

Scan looking from side

I don't really understand the scans but Mr. Thorn said all the round bits and funny shaped bits that you can see are tumours and that the scan is kind of taken in slices.

Mr. Thorn wants me to have a lung scan and if the tumour in my lung has grown then that will have to be removed.

3rd May 2007:
I had to have the lung function test repeated today so the doctor could see how efficiently I am breathing since my last test.

I was asked to put on a nose-clip so that all my breathing took place through my mouth. Then I had to breathe through a mouthpiece attached to a machine that measured the air that I was breathing in and out. I found this really difficult and was asked to repeat the test a number of times. On one of the tests I had to take a really deep breath then exhale as fully as possible to measure my Forced Vital Capacity (FVC); this I was asked to do a number of time because I was not getting the peak that they wanted on the chart. I also did a test where I had to breathe in a special mix of oxygen and carbon dioxide to see how well my lungs were absorbing the oxygen and excreting the carbon dioxide. I then had to go and sit in small chamber for some more breathing tests.

How the lung function test will help
Lung function tests are used to help determine the cause of shortness of breath and other breathing difficulties. They can help to differentiate between different forms of respiratory disease, such as obstructive conditions like asthma or problems caused by infections such as PCP.

I have now been put on the waiting list for an MRI Thorax scan to see if the tumour in my lung has grown.

8th May 2007:
I went for my MRI scan of the brain today. An MRI scan usually gives the clearest scan of the brain and spine. I had to have an injection of a dye, called contrast medium, to make the MRI scan clearer. I was not happy about the injection as when my mum phoned the x-ray department they told her I was not having the dye so would not need an injection. When the doctor came in the room and pulled me from

the MRI machine I thought he was joking when he said I was going to need a needle. So yet again the doctor had problems trying to get the needle in my arm, which left my arm with several bruise's and me feeling really dizzy and sick.

9th May 2007:
Today I was at hospital for a weight check-up and hydro' therapy, I had lost about 3lb in weight so was told that I must start having the Scandishakes everyday as I am not eating so well. Hydro' got cancelled due to a problem with the pool. I am back at the hospital next week.

I received a call to say my electric bed will be delivered tomorrow. I can't wait.

10th May 2007:
Well, my bed came and then had to go back as it was too big for my bedroom, I can't believe it as they told me it would fit. I have now got to see if the OT's can get a smaller bed.

12th June 2007:
I have still not got my electric profiling bed this is all because the OT's ordered the wrong size bed.

I saw Dr. Crompton the Gastroneterology doctor who said my results were satisfactory but wants me to try Docusate sodium capsules 100mg x2 at night to see if that helps with the problems that I am getting. Docusate is known as a 'stimulant laxative'. It acts on nerve endings in the gut wall. These nerves then make the muscles in the intestine contract with more force and more often. When the gut contracts, it moves the contents along faster, and so it reduces constipation. It may also act by softening the faeces.

The tumour in my neck has continued to grow and I have to see this other doctor on Thursday with a high possibility of having to have surgery on it. The tests that I had done on the lung are still inconclusive so I have to have more x-rays in July and at that point if the tumour in my lung has grown then I will need to have part of my lung removed.

My E.N.T appointment went all right too and I don't have to go back until later in the year unless I have any bad ear infection. I still have to continue going for physio' every week, which I don't mind.

Kirsty's Story

15th June 2007:
Thursday did not go so well, I have got to have surgery on my neck, arm and side. I will be in hospital a couple of days depending on how things go as there may be a problem with the surgery on my neck as the doctor is not sure what nerves the tumour are attached to yet. Surgery is planned for when the doctor gets back from her holiday in July.

Mum also received a call to say that Mr. Oxborrow had ordered an urgent MRI scan of my pelvis, which I think is due to the results of the Nerve conduction test. We will just have to see. Mr. Oxborrow thinks I may have tumours in my pelvis too. I have to go for my MRI next week.

1st July 2007:
I had my scan last week and the great news is I did not have to have any needles, which I was really pleased about,

I have also got my new electric bed and spinal mattress so I am managing to get some sleep at long last.

31st July 2007:
I received good news from my lung doctor Mr. P Barber today. He said that my lungs were looking good at the moment and that he thinks it best if he left things alone so does not plan to do surgery for the time being. But he wants me to see a lung Physiotherapist to give me some breathing exercises and see if that will help with the shortness of breath.

Last night I got very breathless so my hospital electric bed came in very useful and helped my breathing tremendously by being able to put the bed head up, which helped relieve my shortness of breath.

14th August 2007:
I have received news from the hospital that my surgery will be on the 29th August 2007, I go in hospital on the 28th August, 2007 ready for surgery the next day. I am not sure how long I will be in for yet but it should only be a couple of nights. I will get confirmation on Thursday when the doctor is back.

I start with physio' on my lungs tomorrow, who said he would try and work it round my other physio' so that I don't have to attend hospital another day for it.

I also received a call over the scans that I just had to say the results have been sent to Dr. Hughes and Dr. Huson who plan to see me on the 12th September 2007 and will then tell me what happens next.

23rd August 2007:
I have been getting a lot of joint pain and bruising for no apparent reason especially on the legs, which I mentioned to my physio' today. She told me to try rubbing or massaging the joints with some anti-inflammatory gel and to try some gentle exercise. Heat from a hot water bottle may also help relieve the pain and stiffness. If things are no better by weekend she wants me to make an appointment with my GP.

I am going to use a Mediflo Duo to help with my breathing, which is a dual use incentive spirometer that can be used for both sustained maximal Inspiration (SMI) and positive expiratory pressure (PEP) simply by turning the product round and re-attaching the corrugated tubing. During SMI, the flow-regulation lid allows the unit to be adjusted according to my functional capacity. I have got to try and use this three times a day.

24th August 2007:
Went for the fitting of my new leg/foot brace's today, I had a pleasant surprise as Mike who I have spoken about before did the fitting, I have not seen Mike for over three years so it was great to see him again. My new braces will be ready on the 26th September, which is the day after my brother's 21st birthday. Mike is an Orthotist. An Orthotist provide a range of splints, braces and special footwear to aid movement, correct deformity and relieve discomfort.

28th September 2007:
My operation went well, I was only in hospital a couple of days, I had four tumours removed altogether under a general anaesthetic, and Mum was able to stay with me. I am still in some pain but that is only to be expected.

Kirsty's Story

I have got to go to the hospital on Tuesday due to having a bad ear infection again and I am at the hospital for my scan results on Wednesday. Still having to go to physio' every week and my breathing is still bad so my physio' is writing back to the chest doctor for more advice.

12th September 2007: Scan and nerve conduction results
I went to see Dr. Huson (my NF doctor) today for the results of my nerve conduction test and pelvic scan results. Unfortunately, the nerve conduction test showed that I do have damage to the major nerves that work my legs and feet, which is why I have developed the foot drop in both feet. The pelvic scan showed that I have tumours all round and on the major nerves in the pelvis.

Dr. Huson decided it would be best if I have a P.E.T scan, Dr. Huson asked Mum and me if I would be happy to have a P.E.T scan and both Mum and I felt that under the circumstances it would be good idea at this stage.

Dr. Huson said if any of the tumours show up as a grade 3 then it may mean a trip to a hospital in London, which I don't really mind if it helps doctors to understand NF a little more.

But it's not all bad news as when Dr. Huson looked at my feet they had not got any worse so my physio' is working well.

Dr. Huson talked about contacting a doctor in the USA to ask if I would be suitable for the drug trial, but I have got two years left at college so we decided we would leave that idea for the time being and see how things go with the PET scan and my foot drop.

26th September 2007:
Today was a long day at the hospital as first I had to attend Hope Hospital to pick up my foot braces that Mike Gilligan made for me

Mike and I go back a long way as Mike was the very first person to make my back brace when I was only 9 years old

After my appointment with Mike it was back in the ambulance for a trip down to my local hospital for my physio'. Mum and I left home at

8am and did not get back home until after 5pm so we were both really tired.

I started being sick again and when I saw my doctor yesterday he said that if it continues I will have to have the camera in my tummy again but in the meantime to double up on my Losec tablets.

30th October 2007:
A lot has been happening recently, the good news being that the recent tumours that I had removed were not nasty. The doctor looked at my foot as I had been getting a lot of pain in it and she said that I have a tumour that is deep into the bone and that it would be a good idea to have it removed, which I agreed with, but not before Christmas as I hope to take my driving test in December. The doctor said that would be ok as long it did not get any worse. She also looked at my tummy as I have been getting a lot of pain around the kidney area so she decided to arrange for me to have an ultrasound scan of my kidneys to make sure I don't have any tumours on them.

I have been having lots of falls recently, I fell down the stairs at home, fell at college a few times and my ankles have been swelling so I have got to see about having a full leg brace.

10th November 2007:
My PET scan went ok, I had to lie in this quiet room for 45+ minutes on my own while the radiation that they injected went round my body and then they took me in the scan room. The scan took over an hour as they scanned from head to toe. They would not let my Mum come in with me, which I was not too cool about as I have never been in the scan room on my own before Mum has always come in with me, I also forgot to take my teddy waaaaaa, I pleaded with them to let my mum come in this other room while they did needle and they agreed to her doing that. I have got two to three weeks wait now before the results are back.

What is PET scan?
P.E.T stands for Positron Emission Tomography. This is a fairly new type of scan. It shows how your body tissues are working, as well as what they look like. The test involves having an injection of a small amount of radioactive material, using the signals from this radioactive injection,

a scanning machine can build up a picture of the part of the body. PET scans can be used to look for abnormalities in the tissues.

PET scans are not a routine test and are usually only used for the small number of patients for whom other types of scans cannot give all the information their doctors need.

1st December 2007:
My doctor is having a meeting next Wednesday over the results of my PET scan and will phone my Mum on Thursday with the results and tell Mum what happens next. My Mum received a call from my GP today asking her to bring me to see her this afternoon. When we got there my doctor called me in and said she had received a letter from my physio' over my knee problem. My physio' wants me to have an MRI scan of my knee due to the amount of falls I have been having, I now have to wear a brace on both knees due to a problem with the ligaments being damaged. My doctor is sending a letter to the orthopaedic surgeon to inform him of the new problem.

The results of PET scan
Mum received an e-mail from my NF doctor, which read:

Good news-there is nothing obvious to worry about. I am about to go to a meeting but will ring next week to go over things and catch up.

>**Sincerely**
>**Sue H**

Today I had to have an ultrasound scan on my tummy/side due to the pain that I have been getting. The good news is I don't have any tumours on my kidney but they found a cluster of new tumours in my tummy in between two major nerves that cross over each other. They are not too big at 1.5 cm in size but with NF tumours it does not matter how big they are they can give you some real bad pain. My doctor will now be informed of the results and I should be told some time in the New Year what they decide to do about them.

2008

4th January 2008:
Mum received a call from my Nf doctor on the evening of the 28th December 2007 to say that she had received a call from the doctor who did the P.E.T scan. He felt it would be a good idea if I had the P.E.T scan done again as he thinks it was a cold day on the day that I had scan and may not have given a correct reading and he is going to use my last P.E.T scan as a base line. My NF doctor wants to see me in February to have a chat over how things are going and to explain the P.E.T scan to me.

22nd January 2008:
I saw my pediatric orthopedic consultant today who looked at both knees; he said that both knee caps were loose but one more than the other and that there was a lot of swelling to the back of knees. He was unsure why and decided it would be better to do an MRI scan of both knees. The hospital phoned yesterday and I have got to go on Friday for the scan.

I also saw my pain control doctor this week at Sheffield Children's Hospital along with other people involved in my care. The doctor spoke about me using flotron boots, which will help to reduce the swelling in my legs, I have worn them before when I was in hospital after my spinal surgery but I think I am going to try support stockings first. We also spoke about me being transferred over to the adult services at my local hospital, which will happen sometime this year.

9th February 2008:
I was at the hospital on Wednesday for physio' in the hydro' pool. While I was there I decided to go and see Pam (the play leader, who is coming to my Ball) but on the way back I was in so much pain that I could not even stand up and was on the floor so a nurse got me a wheelchair. My physio' had a look at me and decided it would be best to put me on two crutches to even me out a bit more. I felt a little better after hydro'

Kirsty's Story

On Friday I went for the MRI Scan on my knees, which only took about 15 min's so it was not too bad.

7th March 2008:
My back and legs have been really painful and I had to wear my back brace for college to try and help with the pain.

I am seeing Dr. Henry on the 1st April when he gets back from holiday so I should get the results of my knee scan then.

My ankle went on me when I was in Blackpool last week. The pain in my ankle was really bad, the foot was black and blue from the bruising. Walking on it was a no, no. The swelling was still bad when I went to physio' on Wednesday, so I mentioned it to my physio'. She took one look at it and sent me off to A/E to have it x-rayed, I am pleased to say there aren't any brakes, just a bad sprain. It's now Friday and the swelling and bruising have still not gone down around the ankle so no driving lesson for me this weekend.

I am going in hospital on the 9th April for an operation on my foot, I have got a tumour that is deep in the foot which is giving some pain when I try to put on my shoes so the doctor said it would be best if they tried to remove it.

There is a small story about me in the Chat Magazine this week, which tells you a little about me and about my fund raising.

24th March 2008:
I saw my NF doctor (Dr. Sue Huson) last week everything went ok really.

Dr. Huson explained that I will be having my PET scan in June as they want to make sure the tumours on my spine and in my pelvis are not growing too fast. If it turns out they are growing I will have to consider having them removed.

Due to the problems that I am having it was also decided that I should be seen every six months but before if I have any new problems.

The pain in my back has been really bad recently but I am due to see

Kirsty Ashton

Mr. N .Oxborrow on the 4th April, the day before my 18th birthday, it was suggested that I should wear the back brace again to help support my back a bit more. But I will see what Mr. Oxborrow thinks first.

1st April 2008:
I was back at Pendlebury Children's Hospital this morning to see Mr. Henry for the results of the scan I had on my knees in February, Mr. Henry gave me the report from the scan, which read:

Both knees, thighs and proximal calf have been included in the scan. There are innumerable neurofibromata of high signal on fluid sensitive sequences distributed alongside the neurovascular bundle of both thighs extending behind the knees and into the calves. Scattered smaller lesions also seen within the muscles and subcutaneous tissues. The larger lesions measure up to 3 cm with a diameter of around 1.5 cm. There is an interamuscular ecognizedas with a diameter of 1.3 cm in the medial head of the right gastrocnemius within the popliteal fossa. Adjoining cluster of smaller neurofibromata is also seen. Multiple neurofibromata also fill up the left popliteal fossa. There is no popliteal cyst seen communicating with the knee joint. No significant effusion seen within the knee joint. No marrow signal changes are seen either. The internal knee structures including menisci cruciate and collasteral ligaments are grossly normal.

After reading the report and looking at my knees again, Mr. Henry told me he would not be able to remove any of the tumours as I may end up worse off. But if the tumours continue to grow the situation will be looked at again and it would be a plastic surgeon who would have to remove the tumours not him.

The report will be sent to Dr. Sue Huson my NF doctor for her to look at and decide if anything more needs to be done.

8th April 2008:
I had an appointment to see Mr. Oxborrow last Friday and after having an X- Ray on my spine; Mr. Oxborrow said the spine has now fused together, which is a good thing. I have been getting a lot of pain at the top and bottom of my spine, which I mentioned to Mr. Oxborrow. The pain does wake me up in the night and tends to get worse throughout

Kirsty's Story

the day. Mr. Oxborrow said it might not be the scoliosis causing it, but maybe my muscle tone.

Mr. Oxborrow wants me to move over to adult services now that I am 18 years old and to do more physio' to see if this will help as he thinks it could be muscular pain that I am getting. He wants to see me again in six weeks to see if things have got any better.

Mr. N Oxborrow also mentioned that one of the screws may have split at the top of the spine and will look into this in more detail.

I don't mind moving over to adults as long as I stay with Mr. Oxborrow, I don't want to be seeing anyone else.

I am going into hospital for surgery on my foot tomorrow, I should only be in a couple of days though depending how surgery goes.

11th April 2008:
I am home from hospital after having two tumours removed, one from my foot and one from my chin.

I had to go on the drip for a few hours as I was being sick, but this is only to be expected after surgery. Everything seems to have gone ok with the surgery and I am not in too much pain now. I go back to the dressing clinic next week to have the stitches removed and the dressing changed.

The doctor said I cannot shower for two weeks (I feel sorry for anyone sitting next to me over the next two weeks).

I have got seven hospital visits over the next two weeks.

25th April 2008:
Everything seems to have gone as well as expected with my recent hospital appointments.

Mr. J Thorn said he cannot do anything to help me at the moment, but if the PET scan shows that the tumours on my spine or anywhere else in the body have started to grow he may have to look at things again and surgery may be needed. In the meantime I have been discharged from his clinic.

Even though I went along to my physio' appointment last week I was in too much pain to do it all so my physio' just did a small amount with me. I just feel so tired recently, not sure why.

My weight has stayed steady so I don't have to take the Skandishakes at the moment, which is great news.

I had the stitches removed from my chin, I think the nurse said I had four and the scar is looking good, I did not have any stitches in my foot so that was a blessing and everything looks to be healing well.

9th May 2008:
My appointment with Mrs. Brains went ok and the tumours that were removed six weeks ago were NF tumours. The doctor also spoke about the scan I had done on my tummy and he said that the results of the scan showed that I had lot of small NF tumours in the tummy, I decided not to have anything done to them unless they start giving me too much pain.

Not having the best of days as when I got home I slipped on the stairs and fell and hurt my back, I was in so much pain that I had to go to A/E. My back was x-rayed and everything looked ok apart from the top of my spine looking a little bent. The doctor I saw said that I should let my spinal doctor know what's happened so he can look at the x-rays too as one of the rods was bent, but I said I think it was like that before anyway. I am due to see my spinal doctor in the next few weeks so I will mention it to him then.

I'm not upset or angry with what I have. In fact, I feel very lucky. There are a lot of people worse off than I am. Mum and I have a wonderful relationship and she's always there for me whatever happens.

I am not frightened by going to hospital, but I am petrified of having needles. I start to feel really panicky even thinking about a needle. I have had so many needles now that my veins just riddle and disappear. I always ask for the numbing cream (Emla), which is put on my arms in a few different areas about an hour before I have any injections.

The cream is covered by a sticky plaster that I like to take off myself as the nurses always hurt when they do it.

Kirsty's Story

Just thinking about the routine now makes me come out in a sweat. The doctor puts the band round the top of my arm and pulls it really tight, and then starts tapping my arm to try and find a juicy vein into which he can stick the needle in the hope he hits the spot the first time. It would be great if it did but it never happens with me. You can bet your life it takes three or four attempts before it's a success.

I know I have got to have many more needles so I am going to get my own stock of Emla cream for my next lot of injections.

21st May 2008:
I went to see Dr. Lieberman (chronic pain specialist) this morning, I first went to see Dr. Lieberman in December 2003, five years ago. If you look back in my diary I mentioned then what a cool guy Dr. Lieberman was and how he made me feel very relaxed when talking to him.

Dr. Lieberman only deals with adults, which is why I was transferred over to Sheffield Children's Hospital for my pain control, but now I am 18 it's better for me to be seen by an adult pain specialist.

Dr. Lieberman is still a cool guy. We spoke about the medication that I am already taking for my pain, Dr. Lieberman said that if the pain got really bad I could take more of the Gabapentin and he also mentioned the possibility of me using morphine patches to help with the pain but I don't really want to start using morphine, I am loopy enough without the help of morphine.

I was also given this new treatment (sorry I can't remember what it was called) where I had to lie on a bed and a sticky pad with wire coming from it was stuck to my hip. The other end of the wire was plugged into a box. The doctor then used an instrument with a wire coming from it that was also plugged in to this box (it looked a bit like a pen with a silver nib). The box was turned on and set to a level that I could manage and the pen instrument was placed over the area of my main pain for about ten minutes. I have got to have this treatment every week for six weeks. The doctor told me it was a very new instrument and that only three hospitals in the UK are using it at the moment. I have been trying to think what it is called and all I can remember it was something like "External neuromal ultra.

I have got to go back and see Dr. Leiberman in about three months to see how things are after this treatment.

I fell off the stage at college this week, which caused some damage to my knee, I was not wearing my foot or knee braces as they need replacing and my knee gave way on me. My Physio' contacted the orthotic services to tell them what had happened and that it was urgent that I was seen to as soon as possible as I have got nothing to support my knees and ankles at the moment, but the earliest I could be seen is on the 11th June unless they get a cancellation.

I am having my PET scan on the 3rd June at Christies Hospital. Having had a PET scan before, I know what to expect this time.

I have been told my weekly visits to the hospital will continue for some time yet, which I really don't mind. My ambulance drivers make my hospital visits fun and I have made so many new friends.

6th June 2008:
The PET scan went well apart from I had problems with the injection again. The nurse could not find a vein and when she thought she had found one after going in with the needle, my vein collapsed. In the end I had to have the injection in my foot. I will not get the results until my doctor returns from her holiday in two weeks.

Busy month with hospital this month, I am also going back to see MR. N Oxborrow, first time of seeing him at the adult hospital. My back has been really painful at the top and bottom of my spine.

14th June 2008:
Hospital is still the same. The new treatment that I am having did not really help with the pain this week as my back has been really bad

17th June 2008:
This was my first visit to see Mr. Neil Oxborrow at Hope Hospital; it felt strange not seeing him at the children's hospital.

Mr. N Oxborrow was not expecting to see me as it was not really his clinic, he was just filling in for Mr. Williamson.

Mr. Oxborrow was still unsure if the rod had moved at the top of my spine but was not too worried about it. He is going to look at my old x-rays and compare them to see if the rod has moved too much. I have got to continue with my physio' and try and do more physio' at home too.

I go back and see Mr. Oxborrow in nine months to make sure everything is ok, but he is going to contact me in the next four to six weeks after he's had time to look over both x-rays.

I could not leave without leaving a gift for his dog even if he did forget to show me an up to date picture of his pet. Talking about pictures, I'm just as bad at remembering. Mum brought her camera with her as I wanted to get a picture of Mr. Oxborrow for my book and web site.

Vicky, My tissue viability Nurse:
Vicky came to see me yesterday so she could measure both my legs for some compression hosiery stockings as my ankles keep swelling up. It was important for the Vicky to assess each of my limbs for suitability for compression treatment before application. Mum went and picked them up from the chemist this afternoon and I found it really difficult to get them on. I am at the hospital for my physio' tomorrow so I will mention this to my physio' as he may have some tips on how to get them on more easily.

18th June 2008:
Today was one of my busy hospital visits as I was seeing Cathy Head, my dietician, I have put weight on, and mum said it's all the chocolate that I have been eating. I then went on to do my dry land physio' with Jane before going on to do some physio' in the Hydro' pool with Gary.

The swelling to the back of my knee is still there and is giving me some pain. My physio's thinks it best if they write back to my orthopaedic doctor and let him know about this swelling as I have had a few falls since my last scan and may have done some new damage to my knee. The knee caps are also getting even more loose and wobbly.

19th June 2008:
My weekly pain clinic visit. The treatment that I am trying for my pain is called External Neuromodulation and is used for the relief of chronic pain.

This treatment was developed at the renowned INPUT Pain Unit at St Thomas' Hospital, London. It targets the nerves responsible for your pain. It changes the behaviour of the nerves so that your pain is reduced. It is normally used for neuropathic or nerve generated pains. These tend to be unpleasant and described by such terms as "burning", "prickling" and "tingling".

What happens during treatment?

A sticky electrode and a metal probe were placed on my skin and a very small electrical current directed at the nerves responsible for my pain. A small amount of gel was used on the tip of the probe.

The treatment lasts about five minutes at each area of the pain. After my treatment, my pain was reduced but this was only temporary. Some patients have got weeks or months of benefit from this treatment and when their pain did return it was with less intensity.

I am having treatment once a week for the next six weeks when things will be reviewed.

4th July 2008:
The pain treatment seems to have helped the pain in my shoulder a little but not the pain in the back. I have got one more treatment to have when things will be reviewed again.

Physio' went ok but I still have this swelling to the back of my knee. My physio' is not sure what it is and is writing to the orthopaedic doctor to ask him to have a look at it. It may be a sack of fluid or a new tumour, she is not sure.

15th July 2008:
A busy week for hospital visits this week as I am there almost everyday.

Kirsty's Story

I have got a bad ear infection again, so my G.P gave me a letter to take to the hospital so that I could be seen in the E.N.T Open Access Clinic. I saw Dr Richard McBride, he said I needed microsuction on both ears again due to the build up of puss and gave me some stronger ear-drops to use for a week. I have got to go back to the hospital next week. Dr Richards also wrote me a letter as I keep getting recurrent ear infection and instead of my GP writing the letter for me to bring up to the hospital I can now use this letter and it will save me time having to go and see my GP first.

16th July 2008:
I received a letter from Dr. S Huson to tell me that the P.E.T Scan showed that that the internal tumours are not growing too fast, which was good news.

I went for physio' in the Hydro' pool this afternoon, Gary, my physio' works me hard.

Kirsty Ashton

17th July 2008:
Today was my last lot of treatment for the pain in my back and shoulder. I have been getting a lot of pain at the bottom of my back, to the top of my back just above the scar and in my shoulder and the treatment is not really helping now. I have got to go back and see Dr. Lieberman in October.

I also received a call from Julie (Mr. N. Oxborrow's secretary) to say that Mr. Oxborrow want's me to have a spinal x-ray done and that I should come into x-ray the next day for it. I am at the Hope hospital anyway having my new foot splints looked at.

18th July 2008:
I went for the x-ray of my spine this morning that Mr. Oxborrow wanted me to have, I also had to have my foot splints looked at as they were not fitting correctly and giving me blister's. They are going to send them away to have some more straps put on at the bottom so my feet will be pushed back into the brace. They should be ready in about ten days for me to pick up.

I have been told my weekly visits to the hospital will continue for some time yet, which I really don't mind my ambulance drivers make my hospital visits fun and I have made so many new friends.

16th August 2008:
I received my new splints, they are a bit bulky around the top of my shoes with the second strap on but my foot is not rubbing as much now.

I'm still attending physio' weekly and in the Hydrotherapy pool every other Wednesday. Having Hydrotherapy helps me with the pain as I find it much easier to move. The pool is quite shallow at one end so I can exercise well within my depth. The temperature of the water is maintained at about 35oc, which is much warmer than the normal swimming pool. The warm temperature of the water helps my muscles to relax and the water supports my weight, which makes it much easier for me to do my exercise and also helps me increase my range of movement. When I do my dry land physio' it's much harder for me to do my exercise.

I went on holiday to Florida for two weeks with my mum and dad, the day after I got back I had to go and see my NF doctor (Dr. Sue Huson) for my six month check-up.

Dr. Huson gave me a good all over medical check. I spoke about how my breathing had been getting worse and about the pain in my back and in my knees, unfortunately Dr. Huson said my foot drop has worsened considerably in the past six months, she is going to contact my GP about all my other problems. But as also decided to send me to see a doctor in London and I may have to see a doctor in the USA due to how things are going.

Dr. Huson said my PET scan was looking good. But that it did show that I have many, many tumours on my internal nerves and that every time they scan parts of my body they find even more tumours.

Dr. Huson also mentioned that she has never seen anyone like me and that I was a one off (mum always said God broke the mould when he made me lol..). I am not sure when my visit to London will be yet as Dr. Huson is away for four weeks, In the meantime I have got to continue with my physio' and do some extra physio' on my feet. I have also been getting very breathless and started being sick again so I have been told to make an appointment with my GP.

2nd October 2008:
Went to see my GP last week and she said that I have an infection and put me on antibiotics for two weeks my GP also took some blood test, can you believe it, I did not have any magic cream on my arm before I had the needle. Don't you think I deserve a cheer for being brave? My mum came in with me thou just in case I wanted to squeeze her hand lol... I went back to my GP yesterday and I still have the infection and have now been put on some other medicine and have now got to go back in two weeks and if things are still the same then I have got to go for a chest x-ray. Next week I have got to see Miss Brains my plastic surgeon over some new tumours that are giving some pain and may need to be removed.

Kirsty Ashton

10th October 2008:
I saw my plastic surgeon yesterday to talk about the possibility of having three tumours removed that are giving me a great deal of pain due to where they are situated, after the doctor had looked at them Mrs. Brains felt it was possible to have the tumours removed without it causing any damage to the nerve involved.

I am busy trying to decide which University to attend at the moment and what I actually want to study, I am looking at going into radio presenting as I use to have my own radio show when I did voluntary work at Wythenshawe FM and really enjoyed what I did at the time. Plus I will be sat on my bum and it will not interfere with my disability too much.

15th October 2008:
I had to see my GP this morning and as I thought I have a water infection (can't stop going to the loo) so I am back on antibiotics. My GP also listened to my chest as I am still getting very breathless and after listening to my chest my GP wants me to have an echocardiogram (or "echo") done. An echocardiogram is a totally safe and painless ultrasound examination and is a quick and easy way to look at the valves and chambers of the heart, as well as the blood flow. It uses high frequency sound waves to form a picture of the valves and chambers of your heart. My GP is also going to speak with the doctor I see over the tumour on the lung to see if I should have the lung function test done again. It was then on to the hospital for blood test (more needles and three attempts before they could get any blood) and on to physio' for my hydro' pool therapy, poor Jane (my physio') just could not get on the frog (float) and kept falling off, I'm cruel when I am in the pool and get everyone else wet who is sat at the side of the pool too. Physio' went well, I was just very tired after.

27th October 2008:
I was called in to see my GP this morning after having had my blood results back from the full blood count that she requested and as we thought the test confirmed that I am enemic so my doctor put me on Ferrous Sulphate 200mg tablets, which I have to take twice a day for the next four weeks and then have a full blood count done again before going back to see my GP and she will tell me if I have responded to treatment ok. I really don't like the idea of all these needles. At

Kirsty's Story

least I now know why I have been feeling so tired and this could also explain why I have been getting shortness of breath and having an irregular heartbeat, which can be some of the common symptoms of iron deficiency. Mum phoned college this morning to explain why I had not been in today and to let them know that I will be in tomorrow but to take into account that I am more tired than usual and that they may find I am less active and that the ability for me to focus is somewhat reduced at the moment.

I have not got the date for my echo test yet but my GP did mention it this morning when I went to see her, so I think she was going to give the department a call.

10th November 2008:
I received the date for my Echocardiogram (echo scan), which will take place at the Cardiac Diagnostic Centre on the 13th November 2008. This is a simple test, which will not cause me any discomfort and I don't have to have any needles, which is a great relief.

Still getting a lot of pain in my back, tummy and legs and I think the tumour in my groin has grown, which I will mention to my doctor when I see her in a few weeks.

15th November 2008:
My echo scan went ok and I was told the results will be sent to my doctor but looking at the scan everything looked ok, which was great news. I see my doctor next week and she will tell me more than.

27th November 2008:
On Wednesday I went for my normal hydrotherapy. I haven't had my physio' in the pool for three weeks as I had to go to Leeds. It felt good to get back in the pool this week as I can do a lot more in water. I spent half an hour in the pool and did all my exercises, which was a bit of walking in the water, my physio' pulling at my feet, trying to balance on this frog and playing ball with my physio'. I felt a bit wobbly to begin with as I have not been feeling so well and still getting very tired at the moment. It did not help matters by me falling at college. My next session in the Hydro' is in a fortnight. My back did ache a lot afterwards this week, and my knees were sore too for a while after, next week I do a dry land physio', which is much harder for me to do and a lot more painful.

Heart scan result:

I don't see my doctor until Monday 8th December when I will get the results of my heart scan and recent blood test. But I'm sure everything was ok with the scan.

I had to have some more blood test, which made me scream when the needle went in, well, it did take a few attempts again before they managed to get any blood, I just don't like parting with it. Some people don't like parting with money, I don't like parting with my blood.

22nd December 2008:

Received a letter over the review on my knee braces, I don't go until 2nd February 2009. But I am going in hospital on the 20th January 2009 for an operation to remove some of the tumours that have been giving me some pain and that doctor said they can remove safely, they did want me in on the 6th January but I have got a lot of work on at college and cannot afford to have time off.

2009

13th January 2009:
I have got to attend the pre-operative assessment clinic tomorrow before going on for my physio' in the hydro' pool. this assessment is to make sure I am fit for my operation next week. I just hope I don't have to have any blood test done, the last blood test I had did not go down so well as the nurse had problems trying to find a vain to take the blood sample.

Things are still the same with my back and I have been wearing my back brace to try and help with the pain, my physio' Jane wants me to see about having a new back brace made so that I can wear it when my back is really bad like it is at the moment. I have also now got the date for seeing Mr. Henry (27th January) over the tumours growing on the back of my knees and me not being able to wear my knee braces due to the braces rubbing on the tumours.

14th January 2009:
My mum and I ended up spending most the afternoon at the hospital, The nurse who did my pre-operative assessment was really nice and we were chatting about Hollyoaks (she likes it too) and after doing all the different test that she needed to do, she decided that I should go for a chest x-ray and blood test. "Yes", I had to have a needle, I thought I was going to get away with it this time. But I am never that lucky. She also decided that it would be better if I came in hospital on Monday, the night before my operation, I asked if I could come after college and it was agreed that it would be ok to come in after tea.

My physio' in the Hydro' pool went ok, but my back is really painful tonight so I am going to put my back brace on to sleep in.

22nd January 2009:
I am now out of hospital after having surgery to remove five tumours from different parts of my body. These tumours were giving me

significant pain and Mrs. Brains my surgeon said she could remove them safely. I have known Mrs. Brains for many years now and she is really good and always has time to explain what she intends to do and what risk are involved with the operation.

The tumours that I had removed gave me a great deal of pain each time I bumped against them; the pain was unbelievable at times.

Before going down for my operation I was told I would need a needle, which is no go with me unless they put some magic cream on the area first, one of the nurses said that it had not been prescribed for me and unless they could find a doctor to prescribe it I would have to have the needle without. My mum said that she would go down to the children's ward and get some for me, mum had not been gone above 5 min's when the nurse came back with some so I texted mum to let her know that I had got some. But that was not the end of my injections, I was given an injection to stop the sickness, injection's to stop my blood from clotting and "yes" they had problems putting the injection's in and "yes" I cried. The next day I told them I did not want the injection to stop my blood clotting as I was able to move about and that I would cope with the sickness by having tablets. I had to stay in hospital a few nights. I have got to go back on Monday for a review of my dressings.

Tuesday I have got to go to the Children's hospital to see Mr. Henry as the tumours at the back of my knees have grown and giving me some pain.

My gran was in the ward over the corridor to me and one of the nurses off gran's ward brought my gran to see me after my operation, which cheered me up. My gran is still in hospital as she is not very good on her feet at the moment and the doctors want her walking a little better with her frame before they can let her home.

27th January 2009:
Yesterday, I had my dressing changed where I have had my tumours removed, the scares look nice and neat so should heal nicely.

I received a lovely bunch of flowers over the weekend from my very good friends, Keith, Pat and Alex.

Kirsty's Story

29th January 2009:
Mr. Henry did not say very much really, apart from wanting me to have more physio', he looked at my knees and said my knee's caps are not stable, he told my mum that one of the tumours in my knee is over 3.5cm in size with lots of smaller one's growing round it. He mentioned that the tumour could of grown and that he did not know how to go about trying to remove the tumour or even if it could be removed so he wants me to see another doctor at the M.R.I hospital who knows more about NF. I don't know when that will be yet. But I hope not too long as my knees are giving me some pain and making it difficult for me to wear my braces.

14th February 2009:
Having a really bad time with my back at the moment, but I see Mr. Oxborrow in two weeks, mum said she will mark my back with a marker so that I can pin point where I am getting most the pain. My foot braces have gone in for repair at the moment and the guy at Orthotics said he will find a different kind of knee brace for me to wear as the ones I have hurt the back of my knee where some of the tumours have grown. He is also going to make me a new back brace so I can wear it when the pain is really bad and don't want to be doped up on tablets. I will not get the back brace until the 25th February though.

My mum's been in hospital too, she had to have an operation on her toe, they fused one of her toes and had to remove one of the nerves in her toe as it had thickened, my poor mum is now hobbling around with a rod sticking out of her toe for the next six weeks.

Then it was my brother's turn at the hospital, mum received a call to say that work had taken him to the A/E department with a bad nose bleed, after four hours in A/E he had recovered and was able to come home and told to take things easy for the next forty-eight hours. What a start to the year, surely it can only get better.

26th February 2009:
I picked up my new knee braces, which felt ok when I tried them on in hospital, but after having worn them for a while they began to itch. Mum got me some long socks to wear under them.

I was also fitted for a new back brace and as I am getting more pain to the top of my spine the new brace will go higher up the back. I have gone for a really cool picture on this brace. Keith, the guy who makes my brace, said I was too old for pictures now, but he knows I'm a big kid and he let me pick a picture. I have gone for a blue background with stars on it.

2nd March 2009:
I went to see my favourite doctor, Mr. Neil Oxborrow, who is my spinal surgeon at Hope Hospital in Manchester about my back. The operation I had on my spine in 2005 did not go without it problems for Mr. Oxborrow as many of you will have read. But recently the pain in my back has been getting worse and one of my hands has started to feel cold while the other feels warm. Mr. Oxborrow said I would need to talk the problems with my hands over with my Neuro' surgeon, but was concerned about the pain that I am getting in my back. Having put one of my last x-rays up on screen, he was a little concerned about one of the screws to the top of my rods and the fact that my spine is curving above where he went up to with the rods. After having a chat with him it was decided that I go back in the back brace to help with the pain when I am in college and when the pain is really bad. He mentioned doing further surgery to extend the rods, which would take them all the way to the top. He said the surgery comes with risk, and as I have so many tumours on my spine he would have to do surgery on my back and then turn me over and do more surgery from the front, which would mean opening my chest.

He wants me to ring him in May and let him know if I want to go ahead with the surgery. If I decide not to go ahead he will discharge me as there is nothing more he can do for me. I really do not know what to do, the pain really kills me at times, but the thought of another big operation also worries me. If I do decide to have the operation I will need to have lots of other test and scans done and I would only allow Mr. Oxborrow to do the surgery. Mr. Oxborrow sent me for a full spinal x-ray so that he could view both x-rays. I had to wear one of those silly gowns that never fit or fashion up at the back, Phil, one of my favourite ambulance drivers had arrived to take me home and seen me in the gown, how embarrassed was I. lol... I knew I would be in for some stick off him. But being a girl I can take it and will give as good as I get lol.

Kirsty's Story

17th March 2009:
I saw Dr. Huson a couple of weeks back, we spoke about the operation that Mr. N Oxborrow asked me to consider having. Dr. Huson was also going to London for a meeting with Dr. Ferner she was also going to have a chat with Dr. Ferner about me and see if she would like to do a video link in clinic. But Dr. Ferner said she would like to see me in person so I will have to go to London at some point to see Dr. Ferner.

I received some notes from Mr. Oxborrow and in it he says that he is a little concerned about the appearance of the top screw and wondered whether that some progression of my NF had caused scalloping around the top pedicle screw. He was going to have my x-rays reviewed at the x-ray meeting.

I am back in the hydro' pool tomorrow, I have not been for a few weeks as I have had other appointments to attend and as my back as been really painful I am hoping the warm water and gentle exercise will help.

I will be glad when my new back brace is ready as my other one is far too small for me now. I was in so much pain that I asked my mum to ring up and see if my new brace had come back and maybe get an earlier appointment but it's still not back.

I have also started being sick again and cannot keep anything down, I am just hoping it a tummy bug and will see how it goes over the next day a so.

23rd April 2009:
I have just spent the last four weeks in hospital due to continues sickness. Mum took me to see an out of hour's doctor who gave me an anti sickness tablet that melts under the gum but they did not help, so I saw one of the GP's at my surgery two days later who said I was mildly dehydrated and gave me some Dioralyte and said I would need to come back if things got any worse, I could not manage to keep the Dioralyte down so mum and dad took me back to the out of hour's doctor two days later, the doctor asked my dad to take me to the A/E department and that he would fax them to say I was on the way.

Kirsty Ashton

When the doctor at the hospital saw me I was put on a drip and told I would have to stay in hospital for a few days, little did I know them few days would lead to four weeks.

During my four week stay in hospital I had some investigation's done to try and find the cause of my sickness, the first test they did was an endoscope, this was done by using a narrow flexible, telescopic camera, which I had to swallow and then they passed it down my oesophagus and into my tummy. I kept being sick while they were doing the test and they kept having to vac the sick away. The results showed that I had some inflammation to my duodenum. But they did not think this was the cause of my sickness. The doctor said that he had taken a biopsy (a small sample of tissue) for testing. I had a sore throat for a while after the test. I also had an ultrasound scan of my tummy this just showed some tumours but they were really small and again they did not think they were the cause of the sickness. I also had a Brain scan, which confirmed I have a brain. But they found nothing to worry about on the scan, which was good news. I also had a MRI scan on my tummy, which showed more tumours than the ultrasound scan did and the doctor hopes to talk with my NF doctor (Dr. S Huson) to see if there is a possibility that one of the tumours are on nerve that is making me sick. One of the doctors suggested that I am making myself sick, my mum went mad with her and told her to ask the nursing staff who had been sat with me when I had been being really sick and one of the doctors had also been in the room a number of times when I had been vomiting. Mum asked the doctor if they would do a gastric study but she just said what did we hope it would show and my mum said, the answer to why she is being so sick. But she refused, saying she did not see the point in having the test. My mum continued to ask if they would just do the gastric test and in the end the doctor agreed to arrange for me to have it. Five weeks on and I am still vomiting over 1000ml a day back, it's not that I don't want to eat and drink, I do, it just does not want to stay down for some reason.

I had a gastric emptying study test done on the 1st May, which will show if my food is going down and digesting as quick as it should (This is the test my mum kept asking for them to do). I would like to thank all the Nurse's and staff on ward F14 at Wythenshawe Hospital for taking such

Kirsty's Story

good care of me and I'm sorry for giving you so many pooook bowls to empty. Mum and dad are running up down emptying them now lol.

2nd May 2009:
I had the gastric emptying study done yesterday and pleased to say I managed to drink the stuff they gave me and was only sick a little bit.

Since I have stopped taking all the anti sickness tablets my sickness is settling down and I have not been sick after every drink that I have.

23rd May 2009:
The hospital phoned on Tuesday to say the doctor had looked at the gastric emptying results that I had two weeks ago and wanted to see me to discuss the results. Mum and I were asked to attend the hospital the next day. After sitting with the doctor and her asking if the sickness had stopped, I explained that things had settled a little, but I was still being sick every day. The doctor then told me that the results showed that I had severe form of gastric emptying and that any food I eat is not moving as fast as it should, which is why I am being so sick, on top of that the doctor said I have so many tumours in my tummy that they are not sure if any of the tumours are on a particular nerve that is making things worse. They want me try Erythromycin, one tablet four times a day for four weeks (this is normally used as an antibiotic, but in my case it's being used to make my food move more quickly), if it helps I have got to continue taking it for another four weeks. But if it does not help after the four weeks, I have got to stop taking it and try this other tablet for four weeks (can't remember what it was called). I go back and see the doctor in eight weeks and if things are still the same they will talk about trying hypno' therapy, if that does not help I may have to have my stomach removed. The doctor said they are running out of medication to try, which is why they think the tumours maybe making things worse. Let's just hope these tablets work and I don't have to go down the path of having my stomach removed.

9th June 2009:
Not much news really, I am still being sick and the tablets that the hospital gave me are not helping at the moment. I am seeing my GP one day next week and will try some other tablets for four weeks and see how I go with them.

I have been busy working on my next charity event. I am hoping to stay overnight in a haunted place. Chris and Pete came to see me this evening they are from the Manchester Paranormal and are going to help me find the most haunted place in Manchester that they can. Many of my ambulance drivers and other medical people involved in my care are going to do the event with me. Channel M filmed me last week talking about the event and hope to come along on the event too. If everything goes to plan I should raise lots and lots of money for other poorly children to have a wonderful holiday.

26th June 2009:
Fingers crossed the plans for my stay in an haunted place are going well, I am looking at staying in Hyde Town Hall, which is meant to be one of the most haunted places that is near to my home.

I am still being sick after having any fluids, I saw my GP this morning due to the sickness my GP is going to have my hospital appointment brought forward, I have also asked for a second opinion, my GP is going to ask for a different doctor to see me. I have also got a really bad ear infection again at the moment, I am at the hospital today to have them cleaned out. I have still not got the appointment to see Dr R Fernere at Guys Hospital yet, my NF doctor said she wrote to Guys before she went away so I should hear something soon.

The pain in my back has been really bad, I am waiting on a scan of my spine to see if I need further surgery to the top of my spine.

12th July 2009:
I had to take my leg/foot braces and back brace back to the hospital last week as they were giving me some problems, they have been taken off me while some adjustments are made and I should have them back next week. Paul spoke about me going in a brace that goes over my shoulders and round my neck as this type of back brace would hold me more straight but I don't want to go down that line as I will not be able to drive with it on. I am sure my other brace will be ok once the adjustments have been made.

Kirsty's Story

15th August 2009:
I have had a busy few weeks with hospital appointments and have appointments almost every day for the next two weeks.

On Tuesday the 14th July I was invited to the Didsbury Rotary Club where I was asked to do talk about the charity that I raise money for, I also took the opportunity to sell some of my pin badges and sold 27 raising £27.00 for the charity.

Physio' in the hydro' pool and dry land physio' as continued as normal and Jane (my physio') works me hard. "Thanks Jane". My ears have been really bad again and after having antibiotic and seeing my GP every week I was sent to the hospital to have them cleaned out. I have to go back to the hospital on Monday to make sure both ears are still clear. I have also had a really bad headache for the past few weeks and my GP has arranged for me to have a Brain scan done. I am still being very sick after having any fluids or anything sloppy, none of the tablets are working. I went back to see Dr. Watts this week, I was told that my sickness was going to be very difficult to cure due to the tumours in the tummy. It was suggested that it could be the Gabapentin that was making things worse until I mentioned that I have been on the Gabapentin for many years and that I had the same problem after my spinal surgery and I was not on the Gabapentin then. The doctor also mentioned that I should have the Brain scan repeated due to my headaches even though I only had one in April, he wants to make sure nothing was brewing on the brain (his words not mine), I told him that my GP had just arranged for one to be done, the next day I received a call to go for my brain scan (10th September), which is when we get back from holiday. The doctor also Spoke about trying hypnotherapy and about the possibility of having surgery to remove my stomach. He did some blood test and also wants me to have a chest x-ray. He is going to write to me next week and tell me what is going to happen next. I was given a new appointment for November. I go to the hospital over my knees on Monday, they are no better and still continue to give way on me. I have also got the date for going to see the doctor at Guy's in London, which again is when I get back from holiday and will let you know how my appointment goes.

Kirsty Ashton

25th August 2009:
I having a MRI Brain scan and MRI spine Thoracic and Lumber/Sacral scan in the next few weeks. I saw the doctor over my knees and he said that both knees are out of line and wanted to do key-hole surgery to re a line them both, but I asked if he could try anything else first so he is going to arrange for me to have some more intense physio' where they wrap my knees up in straps. Could not understand what he was going on about really, but anything is better than surgery.

8th October 2009:
On returning home from our holiday on the 9th September I had to go for a MRI Brain Scan the following day due to the headaches that I have been getting. I have not received the results back from this scan yet. But I am looking at it as being a good thing, if anything was wrong I am sure I would have heard by now. I am still getting lots of headaches thou. I am still having my weekly physio', which is going to be moved up to Warrington so it will make things easier for me and every six weeks I will have physio' with Jane at my local hospital (Jane has been my physio' for the past four years), just so she can keep an eye on things.

I had my spine scan on the 22nd September, the scan was taken of my Thoracic and Lumbar/ Sacral spine, I have been getting a lot of pain in my back, which is getting worse. My mum came with me and she brought some of that magic cream with her, you know the type that helps stop the needle from hurting (I don't do needles) just in case I needed a needle, mum waited in the waiting room while I went into the scan room. The scan started well until they said they needed to inject some contrast dye into my arm. I told them that my mum had some of the magic cream with her and would they kindly put some on before attempting to inject my arm. I have a fear of needles as the nurse/doctor can never find a decent vein to use and when they do, my veins always pop and they have to try again. After the nurse put the cream on my arm I asked if my mum could come and sit with me while I had the injection, but the nurse said I would be ok and that she would hold my hand (I wanted my mum, not the nurse). I warned the nurse that I might scream, shout or even swear and I was saying sorry now before I have the injection, it was no good telling me to be brave that's not helpful. After the nurse had four attempts at trying to get a needle in my arm and my arm looking like a pin cushion I was beginning to get

Kirsty's Story

very upset, they decided to call for the doctor to try and get a needle in after he had tried a further three times he said let me try the back of your hands. I pleaded with him not to go in the back of my hand as although the veins look juicy they riddle and pop, he would not listen and said he needed to get this needle in so that they could complete the scan. My vein did riddle and pop as he went in with needle and by this time I was really upset and just wanted my mum. He decided after having eight attempts it was clear they were not going to find a vein and they allowed me to go and see my mum. The doctor said that he would have a word with my spinal doctor and if he really needs the scan doing with the contrast dye then I will have to come on to the ward while they try and do it.

When I got to the waiting room and saw my mum I just burst into tears again, my arm was beginning to go black and blue from where the needles had been given. After having a hug off my mum I was glad to be home. I am just waiting on the results now. On the 30th September was my visit to Guy's in London to see Dr. Ferner, mum came with me and we were picked up at 7am by ambulance. Jim and Tony were our ambulance guys and they were both really nice and very funny. I had to lie down some of the way as I was in a lot of pain with my back. Dr. Ferner was really nice, we had a chat but unfortunately she had not seen any of my scans, I thought Dr. Ferner was going to tell me if I was a good candidate for the treatment in the USA, but she did not speak about it. Dr. Ferner said I should think about having my spinal surgery in London by one of the NF doctors as if they think any of the tumours on my spine could be removed they would do that at the same time. But I really like Mr. N Oxborrow, he is a great doctor and he's always been there for me and I have so much trust in him, I am going to chat with him when I next see him as the pain in my back is getting really bad. I am still very confused about the surgery on my spine. But if I do decide to have it there is only one person that I would let do the surgery and that's the doctor that's been there for me "Mr. N Oxborrow". Dr. Ferner said she would see me again if I wanted to come and see her again. I may go and see her again but not until she's looked at the scan's. On the way home I was sick a couple of times and Jim and Tony took care of me. "thanks Jim and Tony for being so understanding". On the 1st October I went to see Dr Lieberman at the pain clinic, due to the pain in my back Dr Lieberman's decided to double my medication so instead of

Kirsty Ashton

taking 300mg of Gabapentin 3 x a day I have now got to take 700mg 3 x a day and I go back and see him in four weeks. Next month I am back to see the doctor over my sickness, which is still happening every day, Dr Ferner thinks I might have a problem with my thyroid as even thou I am being sick every day I am putting on weight, I am tired all the time and my periods are very heavy, I am having a blood test next week just to make sure everything is ok. I have my own car now so I can get around much easier and it helps me be more independent. I will try and get a picture of my car on my web soon, so you can all see it. I have called my car "Spike". I have been in so much pain lately that I am keen to get answers and a diagnosis as to why the pain in my back is so bad.

2nd November 2009:
I have now got the results of my brain scan and chest x-ray that I had in September. The findings on brain scan were as follows:

There are multiple small nodules in the subcutaneous soft tissues of the head and neck, and the deep facial spaces, and further in the medial and superior aspects of both orbits. There are possible small mass-like nodules within the cavernous sinuses. There are further multiple bilateral lesions affecting the exiting cervical nerve roots and cervical plexuses. The appearances are in keeping with neurofibromatosis. I had a normal cerebrum, brainstem and cerebellum for age. Normal ventricles and basal cisterns. Normal midline structures and craniocervical junction. Normal major cerebrovascular flow voids. Comments: multiple head and neck subcutaneous soft tissues and deep facial space and orbital extraconal, cavemous sinus and cervical nerve roots and cervical plexus neurofibromas. The appearances are in keeping with neurofibromatosis. No intracranial large mass or hydrocephalus.

The notes for chest x-ray said there were no change from the x-ray I had in January but my doctor said she could not find any notes for chest x-ray in January and I could not remember having one in January. I am still having weekly physio' and this look like it's going to be on going for a long while yet.

I was contacted this month by a lady who had read my web page about me constantly being sick due to having "Gastroparesis", which is delayed gastric emptying, it's a disorder where the stomach takes too long to empty its contents.

Gastroparesis occurs when the vagus nerve is damaged and the muscles of the stomach and intestines do not work normally. Food then moves slowly or stops moving through the digestive tract.

This lady very kindly sent me a link to a story about a young woman who she had read about and that had the same problem as me. She too had tried all the anti sickness tablets and none would help. So she turned to the internet to try and find an alternative treatment. Eventually this young woman stumbled across a pioneering treatment which involves a special pacemaker being attached to the stomach. The pacemaker, which is implanted under the skin, with wires going down into the muscle walls of the stomach. When the patient is eating gastric activity prompts the pacemaker to send a small electrical impulse to the muscles and the gut contracts helping the stomach to move the foodstuff along the gut. The quality of her life has been completely transformed by the revolutionary technique and she hasn't been sick since. I am going to tell my doctor about the pioneering treatment and ask if I can be referred to Robert Macadam, a consultant in upper gastrointestinal surgery, at the University Hospital Aintree, Liverpool who is at the forefront of this pioneering treatment. I may have to apply for special NHS funding as it cost around £10.000, which is what the young woman who had the operation had to do. The operation to fit the pacemaker, which takes around one-hour, is carried out under general anaesthetic. A five inch incision is made above the belly button, and the surgeon then cuts through the fat and muscle and the abdominal wall until they are able to fit the pacemaker, roughly the size of a credit card, directly above the stomach. Electrodes are then inserted into the stomach wall in various locations so they are able to pass electrical impulses and cause the stomach to contract. The first experiments into this type of treatment were carried out in the US but are now available in the UK.

My sickness as been a little better this past week but I am not drinking much as it's when I drink that I start being sick. But this is something worth looking into as it's not as bad as having to have my stomach removed. My weight is steady at the moment, which is another good thing.

9th November 2009:

My knees are really painful and keep swelling up at the moment, I have started some new physio' so not sure if it's this new physio' that's making the knees swell, but will mention it to my physio' when I see her this week.

Mum spoken to my GP last week about the doctor in Liverpool and about the pioneering treatment which involves a special pacemaker being attached to the stomach to stop the sickness and my GP said to mention it to Dr. Watts when I see her and that she would be happy for me to be seen by this doctor in Liverpool, so on my GP's advice that's what I am going to do. While I am not drinking much fluid I am not really being sick very much, some days are much worse than others but I am doing ok.

17th November 2009:

I went to see Dr. Watts last week over the sickness, mum spoke about me seeing the doctor in Liverpool who is doing pioneering treatment which involves a special pacemaker being attached to the stomach, which had been successful on another young woman who has "Gastroparesis", she did not think I would be an ideal candidate for the treatment due to the tumours in my tummy. But my GP said she will send me to see him if want to get some advice off him, The doctor also spoke to me about the brain scan results and she is going to show the results to the neuro surgeon due to the following "possible small mass-like nodules within the cavernous sinuses and the further multiple bilateral lesions affecting the exiting cervical nerve roots and cervical plexuses". They are going to compare the scan with the last one that I had in April and see if these latest results are something new.

Not long off my spook night now, everyone is looking forward to it and I'm sure everyone will have great night as well as raising lots of money for the poorly children. I feel I am back to square one this week with the sickness and just feel really drained at the moment, this week has been particularly bad with the sickness. When my tutor seen me she was concerned that I looked so unwell and I was sent to see the nurse on campus who contacted the out of hours doctor and I was sent to hospital where I was admitted with dehydration again and spent a week in hospital. I came out just in time to do my charity spook night.

Kirsty's Story

2nd December 2009:
I am feeling much better after my recent hospital stay. I was at the MRI l last week seeing the doctor over my knees. He said that I need surgery on both knees and that they will try keyhole surgery first, if I agree. I asked if I could think about it so he's given me three weeks to make my mind up. He was really good looking and I said if he does it then I will have it done lol... But he is the reg' and only assist in the operation's. I asked him to put a comment in my NF book for my NF doctor and told him that doctors normally include their mobile number so the NF doctor can ring them if she needs too, he started laughing lol, well, it was worth a try lol... I go back and see him on the 21st December '09. The operation that I need is realignment surgery to both knees. The doctor was really good and explained that the kneecap normally sits in a groove in the end of the thighbone called the trochlea. When the knee bends and straightens the patella moves up and down in this groove. This movement is termed 'patellar tracking' and if the patella sits centrally on the femur and does not deviate then no symptoms arise. But if the patella has excessive outward or lateral forces then it can move in an abnormal way causing discomfort and the feeling of instability. In severe situations the patella can even dislocate from its correct position and pop out of the side of the knee. This is why both my knees keep giving way. I have decided to ahead with the surgery on my knees and I went for my pre 'op' check on the 19th January. The doctor said the operation will put me out of action for about 6-8 weeks as they are going to do both knees at the same time. The very nice doctor that I saw explained what they hope to do and said they are going to try an arthroscopic 'lateral release' whereby through keyhole surgery the tight lateral structures will be cut to allow the kneecaps to sit more centrally. He did say sometimes this procedure is not enough and needs to be combined with a reinforcement or double breasting (reefing) of the weakened medial structures including some of the quadriceps muscles (VMO advancement). He is not confident that it will work due to how my knees are looking when he bends them, he does not think the tumours that are in both my knees will cause any problems to the surgery, which was good news. He wants to give keyhole surgery a try first before going on to do a more difficult operation where they will have to put screws in my knees to make them stable. The doctor also said if when they start the surgery and for any reason he thinks it will not work, he will stop the surgery and I will be taken back at a later date

to have a different operation on the knees. My knees have got worse and have been giving way a lot more on me. I received a letter from my spinal doctor (Mr. N Oxborrow) to tell me what happened at the spinal scan/x-ray meeting in which my results were reviewed. Mr. Oxborrow mentioned that I have a degree of junctional kyphosis at the top of my metalwork and the scan showed predominately dural ectasia. Mr. Oxborrow is going to send for me so I can talk to him more about the results and does not really know what to do next. He was also unsure if the pain I am in towards the top of my spine is related. I just wish I knew what the pain was then as it's getting worse and I am getting so many headaches too. I am now taking 700mg Gabapentin, 3 x days to try and help with the pain as well as my other strong medication (ketamine) that I only try and take at night as it makes me lightheaded I also received a letter over the brain scan that I had, I am going to see the neurosurgeon to chat about the results.

Apart from being back and to the hospital due to ear infection in both ears over Christmas I have not been too bad and managed to have a nice Christmas with my family.

1st February 2010:
I went for my pre' op' check on the 19th January, I was sat in the waiting room with my mum waiting to be called in, we were messing on my mum iPod touch and mum was trying to beat my score on the game we were playing. One of the nurses called my name who introduced herself as "Heather". Heather was really nice and explained what was going to happen and after taking my medical history the poor woman was going mad and said "I thought you were going to be easy". Heather then said that I needed a blood test encase I needed a blood transfusion during the operation, I looked at mum with my sad eye look (needles and me just don't get along), I mentioned that I have a problem with needles and that they can never find a vein in which to put the needle and when they do the vein always pops. Heather said she would get their best nurse to do injection for me. I went in the other room taking my mum with me so that I could squeeze her hand when the needle went in. The nurse said she could see a nice juicy vein and that it would soon be over, the band went round my arm and made tight so the vein would pop up even more, I held my mum's hand, the nurse put the needle in and started to move it round while in my vein, yes, I screamed, it really hurt,

Kirsty's Story

the nurse removed the needle and said she could not get any blood and would need to try the other arm and again she tried to get blood but was unsuccessful, after looking at both my arms again she decided she was not going to try anymore and that I would have to have the blood test done when I come into hospital as it was something that needed to be done. My arm was left black and blue. I went back to see Heather who still had some more test to do. The nurse told Heather that she was unable to get any blood and Heather said that I was trouble. My B.P taken, which was good, then a trace of my heart, which showed my heart beat was very slow, 55 bpm so I was sent down for a lung function test, which also came back showing my breathing was not so good (I wonder why when I had just been injected twice by needles). After giving a full history of operations that I have had and other medical problems that I have Heather said she would need to speak with the anaesthetist as she was concerned about the gastro' problem that I have, Heather said I could not have a epidural due to my spine and that she had spoken to the anaesthetist who said he wants to make an appointment to see me before the surgery. So I am waiting on that now. On the 29th January I went to see Mr. Leach over the brain scan results, unfortunately I had been very sick during the morning before going to the hospital and felt a little drained. When I arrived at the hospital "Jim" my ambulance driver took me up to the clinic to make sure I was ok. One of the nurses put me in a side room while my mum booked me in. Mr Leach called me in and commented that I did not look so well, I explained that I had been a little unwell before coming to the hospital and that I was just tired. Anyway the first bit of good news I have had for while is that Mr. Leach said I do not need any surgery on my brain and that he could not see any pressure on the brain, he still wants Dr. S Huson to look at my scan and compare it with my previous scan to see if there is any change in the tumours that was found on my optic nerve and soft tissues. It was nice to end the month with some good news.

I have not got a date to see Mr. N Oxborrow (my spinal doctor) to talk about what he thinks should be done about my spine. The top part of my spine is still very painful and I am still getting some bad headaches. If I have not heard from him by the end of March I will give him a call to ask what is happening. He is a very busy man and I don't want to go bothering him at the moment. I am busy now trying to get raffle items for my next charity event and sorting the mobile phone out that have very kindly been sent to me to help raise money towards my target for the poorly children.

9th February 2010:
I received a phone call to say that I am carrying the MRSA bug and that I have got to be treated with two different creams that go up my nose and I have to bath in this liquid soap every day for the next three weeks, I have got to have three clear swabs before surgery can now take place.

MRSA stands for Methicillin Resistant Staphylococcus Aureus. Staphylococcus Aureus is a bacterium commonly carried on the skin. My mum asked the doctor how I had manage to pick MRSA up and seem to think it possible that I picked it up when I was last in hospital in November. I can still attend my lessons and I don't have to be isolated, which is good. I am almost at the end of my treatment now so fingers crossed when I do my swabs it will be clear.

3rd March 2010:

I went to see Dr Watts over the sickness, she now wants me to start taking Domparidon three times a day a long side what I am already taking. Not sure it will have any effect myself, as I tried this medication when I was in hospital for four weeks last year and it did not help then. I mentioned that I knew someone that does hypnotherapy and that I was thinking of giving that ago. Hypnosis is thought to work by altering our state of consciousness in a way that the left hand side of our brain is turned off, while the right hand side is made more alert. For example, someone who consciously wants to overcome their fear of spiders may try everything they consciously can to do it, but will still fail as long as their subconscious mind retains this terror and prevents them from succeeding. I am willing to give hypnosis ago in the hope it will stop me from being sick all the time.

Dr. Watts is going to refer me to the hospital hypnotherapist, but in the meantime I am letting one of my relatives who is a qualified hypnotherapist try and cure me.

My fundraising for the When You Wish upon a Star charity has risen to over £79.000, 00 and I sent 100 poorly children to Lapland in December

Kirsty's Story

2008 to visit the real Santa, which cost £65.000. I am now trying to raise a further £80,000.00 so that I can send 30/40 poorly children and their family on a five day holiday to Centre Parc's with When You Wish upon a Star.

I don't know what the future holds for me, but whatever happens I'm sure it will be interesting. You can keep up with all my news by visiting my website at www.kirstysstory.co.uk and if you can help with my fundraising for When You Wish upon a Star please visit my justgiving link on my website. "Thank You".

The information I have given **should NOT be considered to be medical advice**.

It is not meant to replace the advice of the physician who cares for you or your child.

How mum and dad coped

We are often asked how we cope. So we will try and explain:

You would never guess that our beautiful daughter Kirsty is not a typical healthy teenager to look at her.

But she is battling more than a hundred tumours invading her body.

I feel terrible, because I passed on this rare condition to her and I knew there was a 50-50 chance that it could happen.

I was 10 when I began to notice tiny pale marks on my body, and lumps under my skin.

Kirsty's Story

After having tests in hospital I was diagnosed with neurofibromatosis, where tumours grow on the body's nerve endings. They're benign, but they have to be carefully monitored for any sudden change.

Not a lot was known about the condition when I was diagnosed with the condition, but doctors did say it was hereditary and I had a 50 per cent chance of passing it on to my children. But I had a mild form of the disease and managed to carry on a normal life, so I didn't think it would be a problem.

My husband John, and I started trying for a family and our son Christopher, was born in September, 1986. We were relieved to find that he didn't have the condition.

Then I got pregnant again and our daughter Kirsty arrived on 5th April, 1990.

I was worried Kirsty would have the condition but thought that even if she did, it would be just like my NF and she wouldn't be troubled by it.

I never thought in a million years she'd get it so severely and that it would do the damage it has.

When Kirsty was born I noticed the telltale pale coffee-coloured marks. I mentioned my concerns to the doctors but the doctors said it was too early to tell but I knew. I was shocked, but I thought it wouldn't matter – she would just live life like me. I didn't think for one minute it would be so much worse. When Kirsty was 11 weeks old, the hospital discovered she did have NF1. Kirsty was doing really well up to the age of eight when tests found a curve in Kirsty's spine. Scans showed dozens of tumours pressing on the spine, making the spine bend.

I was absolutely horrified. I hadn't noticed Kirsty's spine was curving and I felt so guilty. She was referred to the spinal unit at Pendlebury Children's Hospital in Manchester but three months later her spine had deteriorated even further.

Kirsty was fitted with a back brace, to give her spine support and keep it in the correct position. She had to wear the brace for 23 hours a day.

Kirsty Ashton

It was tight and uncomfortable, but Kirsty never complained – she put it on during the journey home from hospital and never took it off.

I can't help feeling guilty for what's happened to Kirsty. Of course I don't regret having Kirsty, but I wish things would have turned out differently.

I'd do anything to take her place. Knowing she's in such pain is unbearable. But there's nothing I can do – that's very difficult for a mum to live with.

Many times people have said to me, 'I would never cope if it was my child.' I used to think like that, but one thing you have to learn very quickly is that the only way to get through long days and seemingly even longer nights is just to get on with things as best you can. Some days are tolerable, some not. However I believe that all parents naturally put the needs of their children before their own, Sometimes I would leave the ward, go into the hospital corridor and break down in tears, because I am not able to take away Kirsty's pain. Kirsty helps me so much. She is a very bright, happy child. Despite all the problems she has faced in her life she never complains and is always thinking of ways she can help other poorly children. She is one in a million.

Kirsty is always positive, no matter what maybe happening in her own life, and it's seems that nothing will stand in Kirsty's way, mostly because Kirsty just won't let it.

Kirsty always shows confidence and determination, even in the face of what some would think an impossible task. It's this incredible stubbornness that is evident in everything Kirsty does that makes everyone around her think that they should be doing more for others too.

Kirsty wore her brace constantly until she was 14. Then in March, 2005, surgeons said they would operate and put in two titanium rods to straighten the curvature of her spine.

The doctor said there was a risk of paralysis during the operation and that it was such a big operation that she may not even make it through the surgery, but the tumours were pressing down so much on Kirsty's spine and she was in so much pain there was no choice really.

Kirsty's Story

So on the 10th March 2005 Kirsty went down for the operation on her spine. This was such a difficult time. Every minute seemed like ten, John and I just walked the corridors of the hospital in a daze. We went back to the ward waiting for news. 12 hours is a long time and we were trying really hard to keep strong but I couldn't help thinking about what Mr. Oxborrow said to us and all the risk involved in the surgery. I prayed to God everything would be ok.

Eight hours into the twelve hour operation, the surgeons stopped operating and John and I were both called to theatre. The surgeon met us and said. There have been some problems with the surgery due to the amount of tumours on Kirsty's spine. He had to stop as he was worried that Kirsty may be paralysed. Kirsty was taken to HDU where she stayed for four days unable to move.

The remainder of the surgery was carried out two weeks later, when surgeons tried a different technique to insert the spinal rods.

It was a success but Kirsty continued to be very poorly and was in hospital for three months. She kept smiling through everything. I'm sure she was trying to be brave for me, as she didn't want me worrying. Kirsty was in a lot of pain but was also thrilled that the operation had been a success.

Kirsty spent three months in hospital and I stayed with her, sleeping on a chair next to her bed for two months of her stay.

It wasn't all bad. Kirsty would joke with the nurses and because the hospital was so old Kirsty would tell the nurses the hospital was haunted and play tricks on them, which Kirsty would involve me in too. She would have me get up at 4am and push a car under the curtain towards the nurses station and listen for the nurses' screams when they suddenly saw this car moving on the floor.

Kirsty came out of hospital on the 9th June 2005, which was a Thursday after spending three months on the ward and on the Friday the 10th June 2005 we took Kirsty to the Gentlemen's Night out Charity Committee Annual Presentation, which was being held at the Hilton Metropole Hotel, Birmingham. Kirsty and some other children had been asked to go along with the When You Wish Upon a Star Team to pick up a cheque, which the committee had very kindly donated to When You Wish upon a Star. We all had a brilliant day with lots of surprises. It was a long day and Kirsty was very tired with only getting out of hospital the day before. But when the wish team asked her if she felt up to doing it she did not want to let them down.

The wish children, about six of them, were called to the front of the room and each child was asked what their wish was, and to everyone's surprise including ours the child's wish was granted. I had tears rolling down my cheeks watching Kirsty and all the other children with great big smiles on their faces. The children had suffered so much in there young lives they really did deserve something nice to happen to them.

Kirsty wished to swim with dolphins in Florida, but her doctor said she was too poorly to go at the time so she had to wait a whole year before she was well enough to go.

On the 1st of July, 2006 the whole family flew to Florida for two weeks to swim with dolphins. This was an ultimate dream of Kirsty's that came true after the When You Wish Upon a Star team granted her wish.

The experience was amazing and something we will never forget. To swim alongside these magical creatures and to watch that smile on Kirsty's face you could see the love in her eyes. Thank you to the wish team for making Kirsty's dream come true. The holiday did Kirsty and our family the world of good and we brought back some very happy memories.

Since then, Kirsty has had three tumours removed from her thigh, tumours from her neck, chin, legs, chest area and foot and doctors found more tumours round her kidney area and one in her lungs, which may have to be taken out in the future. Kirtsy is still attending hospital every week four years on but does not let it get her down.

Kirsty just gets on with her life and never moans about it. Doctors don't know what her prognosis will be, and she just takes one day at a time.

She's been fundraising since she was seven. Kirsty and her brother would take their toys into the garden, set up a stall and sell them to raise money.

Kirsty has organised charity balls (with the help of Keith and Pat), raffles and fundraising nights, and raised over £75,000 for the When You Wish upon a

Kirsty's Story

Star charity, which grants wishes for children with life threatening conditions. Kirsty also attended college and studied for a qualification in Performing Arts, to fulfill her dream of acting. Kirsty's now gone on to University to study TV and Radio Production.

How do we cope? Well, Kirsty is such an amazing and strong young lady. I am constantly in awe of how she continues to smile and live and laugh despite all that she goes' through. If only the world could learn from Kirsty; it would be a much better place. She is amazing and we all love her so much.

Having been given a diagnosis of Neurofibromatosis (NF) can be very scary. No doubt about it and I am pretty sure that most of you dealing with the diagnoses of NF have gone home and typed "Neurofibromatosis" into Google, only to become even more frightened from the results that you read on Google.

Let me try and comfort you by saying, the results you get from searching almost any illness or disease on the internet tend to tell you only about the more severe cases.

If you or someone you love is affected by NF, the best way to deal with it, is to find a good support group. This is the best way for you to talk to and share with others who are also dealing with the diagnoses.

People living with NF can live a happy and healthy life. Just start with a healthy attitude. Don't be afraid about the "what if's", them "if's" may never happen.

The way I see it now is that both Kirsty and I both have NF, it's not going to magically disappear one morning and our bodies will be free from this disorder. NF is going to be part of our lives forever, so why not make the best of it.

Kirsty's suffered more than most due to her NF and now she wants to help others by telling them how she's coped with both the up's and the downs that NF has brought her.

You don't have to be afraid, you are not alone and if you need a friend, we are always here for you.

What is Neurofibromatosis?

Many will have never heard of neurofibromatosis, yet alone try and say it. But most people have heard about Muscular Dystrophy or Cystic Fibrosis yet, around 25,000 people in the UK are affected by NF. In fact, Neurofibromatosis (NF for short) is as common as Cystic Fibrosis. Why, you may wonder, is it possible that there is a disorder which affects so many people and yet there is still so little known about it?

A disorder that can occur in any family, affects males and females of all ethnic groups. Nf1 affects one person in every 4,000 births worldwide.

Frequently leads to specific learning difficulties and behavioural problems, affects the body's vital nervous system and can lead to serious complications and, occasionally, even premature death. Well, like everything else about neurofibromatosis, it isn't simple to say what life holds or what will happen next?

There are two different types of neurofibromatosis, 'neurofibromatosis type 1' and 'neurofibromatosis type 2' which I refer to as NF1 and NF2. I am going to talk about NF1 as that is the type of NF that I suffer from.

NF1 is so varied in its effects, and no two people are affected in the same way.

NF1 is a genetic disorder mainly of the nervous tissue. It can cause benign tumours to form on nerve tissue anywhere in or on the body at any time. The signs of NF1 are café au lait marks on the skin, or pale coffee coloured patches. Most people have one or two of these marks but if there are more than six by the time the child is five years old, it is a sign that the child probably has NF1.

Another sign is freckling in unusual places for example, under the armpits, or in the groin area and as a child gets older, tumours (lumps) may start to appear, sometimes just one or two, sometimes lots and lots.

Some of these lumps are soft and can look purplish in colour while others look and feel like peas and these can range from being quite small to being really large in size. These benign tumours are always unpleasant and can be disfiguring, even if they are not immediately apparent on the face or exposed areas. The effect on personal relationships and your self-esteem can be affected. Painful tumours or those that occur in an awkward place can often be removed surgically. But there is always a chance that they will grow back as I have experienced myself after having a tumour removed from my chin that grew back after two years.

What are the signs and symptoms of NF1?
If neurofibromatosis was just a skin complaint, it would have remained a disorder known only to Dermatologists and Plastic Surgeons. But it is much, much, more than just a skin complaint and the complications associated with the NF1 can cause serious problems. The most common of these complications are specific learning difficulties and behavioural problems. But not all children with NF1 have these problems and most have a normal IQ and are outwardly bright and lively but, at school, they may have particular trouble with reading, writing and math's. Unless NF1 is diagnosed early and the appropriate action taken, these children may never reach their full potential.

Having a learning disability does not mean that you are not intelligent. Having a learning disability means that the person has some kind of trouble with a particular subject, which can take many forms, some people may have trouble remembering instructions, paying attention, difficulty reading or difficulty doing math's. learning disability can vary from person to person with NF1, it is important to realize that learning disabilities generally do not get worse over the years.

If you think your child maybe struggling in school take steps to deal with it as soon as possible.

Unfortunately some children with learning disabilities are misunderstood in school, and its thought they are just being naughty or not working hard enough. Talk to your child and listen to what your child is telling you, don't go pushing your child to work harder without first finding out if they have a problem. Many teachers and parents will push the child to work harder, not realising that the child is working as hard as he or she can. There is nothing stopping a person with learning disabilities from going on to college or even University.

The sooner you pick up on the problem the sooner you can get help for your child.

I struggled at school with spelling and grammar and I still do. I have been told that I have Dyslexia. But it did not stop me from going to college and now on to University and even writing this book, I have had help with my grammar but I guess what I am trying to say is, don't give up, follow your dream and don't let NF stand in your way.

Some people with neurofibromatosis will have other complication and the complications associated with NF1 include high blood pressure, curvature of the spine (scoliosis), benign skin tumours called plexiform neurofibromas, internal, spinal and brain tumours (usually benign), speech problems, increased risk of epilepsy and hearing defects all of which can lead to serious difficulties for those affected.

Another sign of NF1 are Lisch nodules. These are very small brown marks that are found on the coloured part of your eye (iris). Over 90 per cent of people with NF1 will have these marks (my mum has these marks on her iris). These marks do not cause any sight problems, but they can be helpful in helping doctors to know if someone has NF1.

Anyone can have a child born with NF1 and that child could be seriously affected by NF1. The reason for this is that NF1 is caused by the mutation of a gene on Chromosome 17. This is no one's fault, it just happens. But if someone with the disorder marries someone unaffected by NF1, there is a 50% chance that each child they have will be born with NF1 depending on whether fertilization occurs with or without the defect as the faulty gene will be present in half of the eggs or sperm of someone affected by NF1. However, even if the parent with NF1 is only mildly affected, there is no way of predicting how seriously affected any of their children will be. Their child may have some serious complications, or may be relatively unaffected; there is no recognized pattern of the disorder and no predictions can be made as to what the future holds

Kirsty's Story

for each individual in the light of how severely the parent is affected. In my case I have NF1 much worse than my mum does.

In 1991, a huge step forward was made and the gene causing NF1 was found, and an effective treatment is now a realistic hope.

After a person with NF1 reaches puberty, small lumps known as peripheral neurofibromas begin to grow on the nerves in the skin. Occasionally they will also grow on nerves that are found deeper in the body. These deeper lumps are called plexiform neuromas and about 50 per cent of people with NF1 will have these. The small lumps can vary in size and shape. Some may be firm and others softer. They can grow as the person gets older.

For some people NF1 is not much more than a skin condition and they may have no idea that they even have NF1. However, for some people the lumps can put pressure on the nerves as they grow and cause various problems.

If large tumours are close to the surface of the skin, they can be unattractive and may be painful if they are knocked.

If lumps are deeper inside the body, they can affect the way that the organs in your body function.

Rarely, do the tumours turn into cancer. Sometimes the bigger plexiform neurofiber may turn cancerous. If you have a tumour that changes, grows, gets hard or becomes painful you should see your doctor and tell him/her that the tumour has changed and giving pain.

How I learned to cope:
Some 25,000 people in the UK suffer from Neurofibromatosis, yet the majority of the population has never heard of the condition.

My Mum found out she had NF when she was 10 years old, she had no idea why her body was covered in coffee-coloured birthmarks or why she had small lumps under her skin.

When mum reached the age of ten, one of the lumps caused her to visit her GP due to the lump giving her some pain. The doctor assured my gran (mum's mum) the lump was nothing to worry about, but as mum

Kirsty Ashton

and gran were going out of the door the doctor asked if mum had any brown marks on her body, to which my gran said "Yes, loads on her back". Mum was then sent to the hospital to have a biopsy done on the lump and it was at this point mum discovered she was suffering from Neurofibromatosis (NF1).

The hospital doctor told my gran that mum had Neurofibromatosis (NF1) and that it was hereditary. Gran said that no one on her side of the family had NF1, but looking back mum's dad may have had NF1 as he had small lumps all over his face.

Gran divorced from Mum's dad when Mum was only little and when Gran contacted him to ask if he had NF1 and to explain that his daughter had just been diagnosed with the condition and that doctors asked if they could have a word with him, he refused and said that he didn't have it and would not help the doctors. Gran never spoke to him again after that. Over the years mum's had a few small nodules and some larger lumps, called neurofibromas, under her skin removed due to them giving her some problems. Mum said: the lumps she has now are just there, but being attached to the nerves if she knocks them she can get pain. When mum was first diagnosed she use to think, Why me? Why should I be different? Nearly 40 years ago, very little was known about NF1

With me if the lumps grow so much that they are severely affecting my nerves and giving me pain, an operation is performed which gradually cuts them away. I have lost count of how many such operations I have had. I just hope the lumps do not grow back, which they can.

Mum and I both have six monthly check-ups to monitor our condition with an NF doctor.

People say to me, "how do you cope?" And I say, "You just have to get on with things." I ignore it and try to shut it out and get on with life. That's the way I handle it.

I may have NF but NF does not have me and I'm pleased to say my brother does not have NF.

Kirsty's Story

Treatment and therapy
There is no cure for NF but the Neurofibromatosis Association is optimistic that there will be an effective treatment within the next 5-10 years.

Sometimes surgery may be necessary to remove some tumours (such as acoustic neuromas or brain tumours) and this can cause complications such as facial paralysis.

MEDICAL FOLLOW-UP FOR NF1
NF1 can cause life-threatening problems, but fortunately these are rare.

The majority of people who have NF1 go through life with very few medical problems, which are related to NF, and enjoy good health.

But it is important to have regular medical follow-up, in order to catch any of the health problems that NF can bring as early as possible.

It is a good idea, to see a doctor who is familiar with the disorder at least once a year or more often if a particular problem is spotted. The doctor can be your family doctor or may be a specialist who deals with neurofibromatosis. You should use these visits to ask any questions you might have about the condition, and to talk about any changes you have noticed in your body. It is especially important to tell the doctor if you are in pain, experiencing numbness or tingling noticed sudden growth of any of your Neurofibromas, getting headaches, or noticed any new neurofibromas.

Usually, your doctor will be able to reassure you with a simple examination. Sometimes the doctor may request special tests to be done to check out any symptoms you may be experiencing. This is important in order to catch problems as early as possible. Whether you've got NF or not, it can be alarming to find a tumour. There's no point worrying in silence, so check out any changes with your doctor and, remember, many tumours turn out to be benign and harmless. Even in awkward places, so it's important to keep an eye on tumours and see a doctor regularly to check they're not turning nasty.

Kirsty Ashton

Help and support for NF sufferers:
Most signs of NF1 appear during childhood or adolescence, and signs of Nf2 appear during the 20s. Discovering you, or someone you know, has got NF can be a bit of a shock, but there is help and support available for NF sufferers in the UK.

Organizations such as the Neurofibromatosis Association can provide help and information about the condition.

Couples with a family history of neurofibromatosis who are thinking of having a baby can be referred to a genetics specialist before getting pregnant, for advice. However, neurofibromatosis is unpredictable – how mild or severe a parent's case is has no bearing on how the child will be affected or what complications they may have.

Unfortunately there's still a lot we don't know about neurofibromatosis. It's an unpredictable condition – there's no way of knowing exactly how it will develop for you, and how your café au lait patches will look in coming years.

There isn't any medical or surgical treatment that can cure or reverse the condition. In fact, a major focus of research is to try and develop effective therapy. The best that doctors will be able to offer at the moment is to keep a close eye on you and look out for any signs of complications.

It is normal to feel angry and overwhelmed at times as you face the uncertainty that NF brings. You must learn to live your life, and not let NF rule your life. The more you understand about the condition the more you will be in control, so be sure to ask questions of your parents, teachers, and medical professionals. Find someone you trust, and share your feelings, fears and frustrations with them. The challenges posed by having NF are hard, but they can be overcome

If you have recently found out that you or a member of your family has NF, please don't worry, I'm here to help and support you in any way I can. You may feel you are alone right now, but you're not.

Please go to my web address at www.kirstysstory.co.uk and send me an e-mail or leave a message in my forum and I'll get back to you as soon as possible.

If you or somebody you know suffers from Neurofibromatosis don't worry.

Together we can help each other.
The Neurofibromatosis Association Quayside House
38 High Street
Kingston upon Thames
Surrey
KT1 1HL

Neurofibromatosis Question and Answers

You may have just learned that you have neurofibromatosis, or perhaps you have been going to doctors for years because of the disorder and living with more serious complications.

Neurofibromatosis can affect the body in many ways, and it can affect different people in very different ways. In some it may be nothing more than a nuisance, but in others it can cause important medical problems. It is natural to have lots of questions when a person is told that he or she has a condition such as neurofibromatosis.

Below are some of the questions that I have been sent over the years, I hope these answers help you if you have NF.

Q: Does NF remain stable over a lifetime or does it get worse as we get older?

A: NF1 and NF2 are both progressive disorders, but the rate of progression and any complication are very much unpredictable. A person with NF1 may experience an increase in the number of neurofibromas that they have over his or her lifetime.

Q: Is there a cure for NF?

A: The simple answerer is "NO", but there is researchers worldwide working to find more effective treatments that will help people with NF.

Q: Is there any research being done for NF?

A: Yes, research is being carried out all the time.

Q: Is NF the same condition as the Elephant Man had?

Kirsty's Story

A: No, but for many years doctors believed that Joseph Merrick (the elephant man), had NF, then in 1986 it was proved that Joseph Merrick had an extremely rare condition called Proteus Syndrome and not NF.

Q: Does NF occur more in men or women?

A: NF affects both women and men of all races equally.

Q: Can someone with NF still donate blood?

A: Yes, people with NF can donate their blood, and anyone who receives their blood will not develop NF as a result of receiving blood from someone with NF.

Q: Is NF an inherited condition only?

A: No, 50% of cases of NF will have been inherited from a parent who has NF. The other 50% of NF cases are a result of a spontaneous mutation in the sperm or egg cell.

A person affected by NF has a chance of passing the condition on with every pregnancy they have.

Q: If I think I or someone I know may have NF what should I do?

A: for anyone who thinks they may have NF they should first see their family doctor who will then put them in contact with a doctor who is more knowledgeable about NF who will then discuss your symptoms and concerns with you.

Q: what is the difference between NF1 and NF2?

A: if two or more of the following are present, a diagnosis of NF1 is normally confirmed.

- Family history of NF1
- Freckling under the arms or in the groin area
- Six or more light brown café-au-lait marks on the skin (these look like birth marks)
- Small pigments on the eye's iris, which are called "lisch nodules"
- Small bumps (neurofibromas) on the skin

Kirsty Ashton

- Skeletal abnormalities, which is bowing of the legs, curvature of the spine (scoliosis) or thing of the shin bone
- Optic Glioma

With NF2 if one or more of the following are present a diagnoses of NF2 is likely.

- Family history of NF2
- Tumours found on both the auditory nerves, which may cause deafness, balance problems or ringing in the ears
- Tumours can be found on the brain, meninges or spinal cord
- Pre-senile cataract
-

Q: What is the prognosis for someone with NF?

A: in most cases the symptoms of NF1 are mild and the person can live a productive life. But in some case, however, NF1 can be very debilitating and unfortunately no doctor can say how you maybe affected by the NF.

Q: Should I tell my child teachers that my child has NF? I don't want my child to be labelled as having a learning disability.

A: Yes, it's always advised that you tell your child teachers that your child has NF as this will help to lead to earlier detection and treatment of any learning problems your child may have due to NF.

It is very important to recognise learning disabilities and to take steps to deal with them as soon as possible. Unfortunately some children with learning disabilities are misunderstood in school, and thought to have bad behaviour, or not be working hard enough.

Some teachers may try and push the child to work harder, not understanding that the child is working hard, but they are just unable to perform certain task as well as they can others.

A person with NF can go on to college and even University with the special help and support they need.

Kirsty's Story

Just remember you are not alone. I welcome everyone who visits my website and I look forward to many new friendships and helping many more people with this unpredictable and cruel condition.

What is Scoliosis?

Scoliosis (sko-lee-oh-sis) is a Greek word, which means 'crooked' and is a deformity of the spine.

Scoliosis is not a disease, it's not contagious and it does not develop due to anything the child or its parents did or failed to do. It just means that in an otherwise healthy child the spine has curved or twisted.

A curvature of the spine can sometimes have two bends, which is a double curvature resulting in your spine looking like an "S" shape. An "S" shape spine can lead to discomfort and breathing problems as the lungs and heart can become compressed.

Scoliosis is much more common in girls than it is in boys and can develop at any age, but is more common when the reaches adolescence.

Causes of Scoliosis

There are two types of scoliosis, the first being "Idiopathic" and "syndromatic".

Idiopathic means "for no known cause" Syndromatic relates to the result of another disease. In adults, this cause could be due to degenerative changes in the spinal column.

Scoliosis is often found in patients who suffer from cerebral palsy or Spina Bifida. It can also be found in patients who suffer from neurofibromatosis due to problems with their bones.

Symptoms of Scoliosis

There are many symptoms with scoliosis and sufferers may present with one or all of the symptoms.

The shoulder blades can look uneven and unevenness to the hips and waist is a common symptom, accompanied by a leaning of the body to

Kirsty's Story

one side if any of these symptoms are obvious, your doctor will perform a thorough examination and the diagnosis will be confirmed with x-ray or scanned images of the spine.

An "S" shaped curvatures is harder to see by just looking at the back as the two curves can counteract each other. However, the curves are very obvious on an X-ray. You don't normally feel pain with scoliosis, more of an ache but pain can develop later on if the scoliosis worsens and is left untreated. The chance of progression is more likely if the curvature is in the upper part of the spine.

Many doctors will ask you to bend over and touch your toes as this will also show a raised hump on your back.

Treatments for Scoliosis

Treatment can be varied from patient to patient.

In young children if the curve is only mild, it will often be left without any medical intervention, but the child will be monitored regularly for signs of the scoliosis getting worse.

In some cases the doctor may decide to use a back brace for children who require treatment, as their bones are still growing and it's hoped by using the brace it will retrain the spine to follow a new path of growth.

The back brace will also help support the still developing spine and hopefully help prevent the scoliosis from getting worse. The brace must be fitted by a specialist.

Spinal surgery is only done if the curvature is causing problems with nerve compression, which results in numbness or tingling in other parts of the body.

Spinal surgery (spinal fusion) is very complex surgery with the possibility of many risks.

Scoliosis is a common condition that may or may not need medical intervention. Any treatment needed must be thoroughly discussed between patient and Doctor to ensure the correct choices are made

Kirsty Ashton

for each individual person. Psychological and emotional support is equally important for sufferers, especially in the cases of the more severe deformities.

If you suspect your child may have scoliosis, please visit your family doctor, as diagnosis should be made by a doctor after thorough medical examination.

When I had my rods inserted in 2005 I couldn't wait to go on holiday as I wanted the airport metal detectors to go off, I know I'm being "bad" but it would have been fun. (The titanium rods don't set the airport metal detectors off or any other forms of security alarm).

What is a Boston Brace?

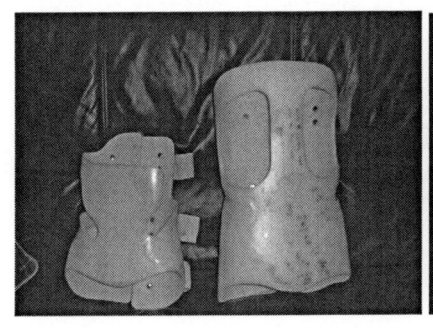

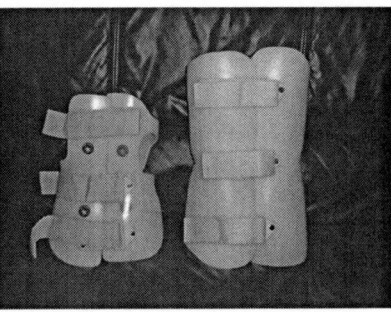

Front view   **Back View**

Bracing is commonly prescribed to prevent progression of the spinal curvature. There are several types of braces used for scoliosis but if you have to wear one it will depend on the individual's condition and type of curve as to which type of brace you will have to wear.

The Boston brace, is the one I am going to talk about as this is the brace I had to wear. The Boston brace is a light-weight brace that can be worn under the clothes and made from plastic.

The brace will need to be carefully made for your child and to do this a cast of your child's back will need to be made (a mould). This is done during an out-patient appointment, but you will have to make a few trips to the hospital

On the left is my first brace from when I was 8 years old. If you look at the back view of the brace you can see the straps made from Velcro, which go through the metal loop to the right and are pulled really tight.

When I go and see Mike, he checks out how my brace is fitting and how I am doing. When I first got the brace, I had to go a few times to get everything adjusted.

The larger brace is about my fourth brace to be made so this shows you how much I have grown.

Does the brace hurt?

No, not really. But sometimes I get hot and itchy. I wear a T-shirt /vest under it to stop the brace from rubbing against my skin. But sometimes wearing a T-shirt/vest under my brace, and then a regular shirt, makes me feel very hot.

Are there activities you are not allowed to do?

"Yes" gymnastics, because you twist and turn too much.

Goal:

To be wearing the brace 23 hours a day by the 8th to 10th week of getting your brace. This will require help from a loved one.

1. Your brace must be put on correctly.
2. Skin must be looked after to stop it from getting red and sore.
3. Your brace must be kept clean.

Having the Brace put on:

To put the brace on properly really takes two people, the wearer and the helper. Always wear an undershirt under the brace with your underpants going over the brace.

Some simple steps I had to follow:

- I had to stand up while the person helping me stood behind me while holding the brace in their left hand.
- My helper then put the brace in front of me with the opening at the back.
- My helper then reached around me and spread the brace wide enough so that I could then step into the brace.
- You have to make sure you have all the straps outside the brace.
- The opening on the brace had to be in the middle of my back so that the bumps down my spine and the crease between the buttocks are halfway between each edge.

Kirsty's Story

- I then had to bend at the hips and knees by about 45 degrees. I then held my hands on my hips and with hands on "hips" of the brace, push down on the brace, so that the sausage-shaped pads on the inside of the brace fitted above my hip bone.
- It was very important make sure there were no wrinkles in my undershirt. Wrinkles could have caused sores on my body as well as being very uncomfortable for me.

The straps had to be pulled as tightly as possible by my helper. Then my helper threaded the straps through the buckles to fasten.

Skin care:

The skin under the brace needs to be toughened. The skin can become very red, and raw. Following these steps helped prevent that. I had to do the following twice a day.

- Bath or shower.
- Rub surgical spirit to all parts of the skin the brace covered as this will helped toughen the skin.
- Always wore a cotton undershirt (without seams), Mum turned the shirt inside out so I didn't have the seams pressing on my skin.

STAGE 1: this is information, which may help you if you have to wear a back brace. Try to wear the brace for 6 hours.

- Apply the brace properly and wear it for around 2 hours. Take it off and check your skin and give your body some skin care by applying surgical spirit on to your skin.
- If the skin is pink, put the brace back on for 2 more hours then check the skin again. Do this again for half hour then put on again.
- If your skin is looking red or sore, the brace must be left off for about an hour and then put on again.
- If you are still at school like me you can easily do this after school.

Do this for the next 2/3 weeks.

STAGE 2: try and keep the brace on for 10 hours.

- If you have managed stage one then you are ready to move on to next stage. This can be a little difficult to accomplish during a school day so try doing this over the weekend.

Start by putting brace on for 4 hours. Then check the skin and give some skin care. Put brace back on and in 2 hours check the skin. Repeat this every 2 hours until you have worn the brace for 10 hours. This stage can last a few days. Move on to stage 3 when you are comfortable to do so.

STAGE 3: Wear brace 18/23 hours a day.

- Now try and wear the brace for school and at lunchtime. Take the brace off and check your skin and give some skin care. Put brace back on again. You will need help for this.
- When you get home take off the brace have a bath or shower, give skin care and put clean undershirt on before putting the brace back on.

This may take many weeks, but don't worry and take your time.

EXERCISES: There are two sets of exercises that I was given.

- One will be a set for you to do during the hour you are not wearing the brace. These will help your back and stop your muscles from getting weak.

The second lot of exercises are those which you do while you are wearing the brace. These should be done as often as you can during the day as it's these exercises, which will help your brace to be more effective in the treatment for your scoliosis.

CLOTHING:

It is best to wear loose fitting clothes over the brace. Pants usually have to be two sizes larger. You are best buying pants with an elastic waistband as they tend to fit more easily.

Kirsty's Story

I have been in my brace for 6 years now, wearing it for 23 hours a day and I will tell you one thing. It keeps you warm in the winter.

The brace I wore after surgery is slightly different, the main difference is that you fasten the brace at the front, I found it more difficult to bend in this brace but that could be down to the surgery. This brace is also worn up to six months after surgery depending on your situation.

The brace needs to be worn 23 hours a day, with relief during bathing and exercise only.

The Boston brace is a moulded brace, which comes up to beneath the underarms and is fitted to be worn close to the skin so that it doesn't show under clothes. It appears to be effective for mid-back and lower curves. In one study treatment was judged successful in 61% of adolescents who wore the Boston brace, and success correlated with wearing the brace more than 18 hours a day. Wearing them for 16 hours a day may still be beneficial, although the risk of curve progression is significantly higher the less time the braces are worn.

The brace does come with its problems. It is hot to wear and can reduce lung capacity by nearly 20%.

Wearing the Brace is not always effective, and patients may require surgery even after being braced.

The facts about my condition from my doctors

I asked my spinal doctor (Mr. Neil Oxborrow), my NF doctor (Dr. Sue Huson) and my neurosurgeon (Mr. John Thorn) to explain some of the medical facts about my condition.

Mr. Neil J Oxborrow
My spinal doctor

I first met Kirsty in 2004 by which time Kirsty had already seen enough doctors to more than fill her notes with correspondence. At this time the neurofibromatosis had caused her spine to curve to one side (scoliosis). Scoliosis is quite common in neurofibromatosis and often the curves can progress rapidly. Kirsty had already been seen at this stage by the neurosurgeons as she had pain in her legs from lumps forming on the nerves as they came out of the spine (neurofibromas). It was felt by the neurosurgeons that nothing really could be done for the pain as they could not be sure which of these lumps was actually causing pain.

We discussed in detail what an operation on Kirsty's spine would mean and decided to proceed. On the 10th March 2005 Kirsty was brought into hospital initially to have an operation on the front of the spine. To gain access to the front of the spine involved making a cut along Kirsty's side and taking out a rib. When we got to the front of the spine we found that it was covered in neurofibromas and the disease was very extensive. During spinal surgery we monitor the function of the spinal cord to make sure that it carries on working well throughout the procedure. Any surgery on the spine carries a small risk that the spinal cord doesn't like what we are doing and at worst this can mean that some patients can lose the use of their legs. This is a very rare complication. Halfway through the operation the monitoring started to suggest Kirsty's spinal cord was not happy. In this situation we do not take any chances at all and we stopped operating, sewed Kirsty up and woke her up. We all breathed a sigh of relief when Kirsty woke without any problems in her legs.

The safest thing to do is to wait a period of time and then take the patient back to theatre to finish the operation. As we had already done quite a lot of the operation at the front and taken out a lot of Kirsty's discs (bits of gristle in between the bones of Kirsty's spine) we thought it simply best to do the second operation from the back rather than go in from the front of the spine. Kirsty was then taken to theatre for a second operation on 25th March 2005.This time everything went without any cause for concern.

Although the spinal side of things was now fine Kirsty had significant problems with sickness after the operation and was really quite unwell with continued nausea and vomiting. This was so bad it meant Kirsty was losing quite a bit of weight. In the end she was transferred under the care of one of the medical doctors for further management until this settled down. Kirsty has continued to get significant back pain after surgery and has also had problems from other neurofibromas affecting nerves in her legs, thighs and really the extent of Kirsty's disease is such that much of this pain and many of these problems are not really amenable to treatment. It is important for us to keep an eye on these neurofibromata to make sure none get particularly big or painful as this can mean this turns into a more nasty form of growth or tumour.

Despite continued pain Kirsty never ceases to come to clinic with a smile and has had to be banned from bringing presents of squeaky toys for my dog as the noise at home was becoming unbearable.

Her latest pain would be well above the area that was previously operated on and we are currently thinking about whether further surgery may be of benefit. The pattern of Kirsty's pain is very difficult to be sure of, however, as it has always been difficult to know how much of the pain was coming from the neurofibromas which we cannot do anything about and how much may be coming from something we could do something about.

Dr. Sue Huson
My NF doctor

Neurofibromatosis type one (NF1): the genetic condition underlying Kirsty's medical problems Sue Huson MD FRCP, Consultant Clinical Geneticist Neurofibromatosis Centre

Regional Genetic Service Central Manchester Foundation Trust.

'Neurofibromatosis what's that? It's a real jaw breaker of a word!' said one of my new patient's Dad this week. From a medical perspective we use Neurofibromatosis as an umbrella word for a group of genetic conditions that cause benign tumors to grow on nerves (neuro-). Under the microscope these contain fibrous tissue (fibro-) and multiple tumors may develop (-osis). Kirsty and her Mum have the most common form, type one (NF1), which affects about one in every 2500 babies born. This is as common as Cystic Fibrosis- so why is NF1 not a household name? The reason is that it affects people very differently, even in families, and for many people it is just a skin condition not associated with major medical problems. Even when it does affect people seriously it can do so in many different ways- I have been running an NF1 clinic for nearly 20 years and have only met one or two other people with the combination of NF1 related problems Kirsty has.

What causes NF1?

NF1 is caused by a spelling mistake in one of the genes (called the NF1 gene).

We all have two copies of every pair of genes- we get one from our Mum and one from our Dad. People with NF1 have a spelling mistake (referred to as a mutation) in one of their NF1 genes. About half the people with NF1 inherit it from their Mum or Dad. The others are the first people in their family to have NF1- in them the spelling mistake happened either as the egg or sperm were made or very early in their development. When people with NF1 have children there is a 50:50 or one in two chance of passing it on.

Kirsty's Story

How does NF1 affect you?

I find it easiest to think about this in two ways- first, to look at the things that develop in nearly everyone with NF1 and then to look at what I will refer to as NF1 complications, the things that only happen in some people.

The main way NF1 shows itself in children is by flat brown marks on the skin, called café au lait spots (they are coffee coloured and were first described by some French doctors). Some may be present at birth but it is more usual for them to begin to show in the first year or two. All of us can have one or two of these spots but people with NF1 nearly always have more than six. The other main thing that everyone with NF1 develops is the neurofibromas themselves- they are small purplish lumps on the skin. They begin to develop anytime from around ten years of age. The numbers that develop are very variable but when people have a lot they can be a major cosmetic problem. Fortunately they mainly grow on the skin of the trunk so when you meet people with NF1 there are usually no signs you would see when they are dressed.

What makes NF1 difficult?

If all people with NF1 got were the café au lait spots and skin neurofibromas it would be thought of as a skin problem and nothing else. The problem is people with NF1 are at risk of a long list of complications. Most of these can occur in any one of us, it is just that in people with NF1 there is a higher chance. For example, about half the people with NF1 struggle with their learning at school. This is the most frequent complication, the next most frequent are related to more complicated neurofibromas than the small ones on the skin. Some people develop neurofibromas which grow very large called plexiforms and these can be a major cosmetic problem. Other people develop neurofibromas on the internal nerves and if these cause pressure on the nerve it can cause problems with nerve function.

The other complications all affect far fewer NF1 patients but the list of what can happen is long and can affect almost any part of the body. This causes a real problem for people with NF1 and their Doctors- we don't have good ways of predicting how NF1 will affect people and the variability means we can't offer screening tests that will pick up every possible problem. This uncertainty with NF1 is one of the most difficult things about living with it, things can crop up at any time- the chance of bad problems are still small but bigger than they are for other people. The best description I have heard of this comes from a man with NF1 interviewed by Professor Joan Ablon (Ablon 1992) – she spent several years talking to people with NF1 to find out how they coped with the condition.

'Most diseases will unfold in a certain way – slower or faster. With NF1, because the symptoms are so unpredictable and variable, you don't know whether there will be symptoms, what they might be, or if they will be serious. You never get your balance or equilibrium how to deal with them. After one thing appears and you deal with it, here comes another. It is not just that there are big and little fires, there is always the worrying sign up that says 'Danger of Fire'. The psychological burden is always there, regardless of the extent of the physical problems.....'

NF1 and Kirsty

Kirsty's Mum has NF1 but for her it has mainly been a skin problem. In turn, Julie had inherited NF1 from her Dad but her parents split up when she was only three and she doesn't know much about her Dad's NF1. Kirsty and Julie show exactly how variable NF1 can be- for Julie it has been a skin problem and she has needed a few skin lumps removed from time to time. For Kirsty, ever since her scoliosis was picked up when she was eight NF1 became a bigger issue. The curve of her back gradually got worse and she needed an operation to stop things getting worse at the age of fourteen. It was then that a further problem became obvious- Kirsty is someone whose neurofibromas are growing mainly internally and not on the skin. So while I have known Kirsty we have realised she has them on most of the nerves as they leave her spine and on many of the big nerves in her arms and legs. There is no way these can all be removed without causing major nerve damage and so we have to carefully monitor her and only remove the neurofibromas if they grow particularly big and press on a vital organ like the spinal cord. The tumours Kirsty has are beginning to cause her nerves not to work properly, she has developed weak ankles with foot drop and her knees keep giving way.

The frustrating thing is we have no medical treatments which will stop this progression. Although Scientists are working hard to understand NF1 and this work is now identifying drugs which may shrink NF1 tumours, clinical studies are only just beginning. We hope that over the next two decades we will find successful drug treatments for NF1.

How Kirsty copes with her NF1

It is a real privilege to know Kirsty and her Mum Julie. Some people faced with severe health problems affecting their mobility and making them easily tired, would have found it easier to 'give in' to their NF1 and not do very much. Not Kirsty- every time I meet her there is always some new fund raising venture on the go or she has been talking to someone with NF1 about how she copes with it. Kirsty is a great ambassador for NF1 and for all children with chronic health problems. Keep up the good work!

Kirsty Ashton

Mr. John Thorne
My neurosurgeon

My name is John Thorne and I am a Paediatric and Adult Neurosurgeon working both at Royal Manchester Childrens Hospital and Salford Royal Hospital. I have been involved in Kirsty's care now for many years and my main involvement with her has been in the discussions around whether or not the Neurofibroma's in her lumbar spine would benefit from excision. Kirsty first presented with very severe pain and dysfunction and MR imaging of her spine showed that she had many lesions on the nerve roots of her lumbar spine, but in particular one large one.

This large Neurofibroma was possibly causing her progressive symptoms, but resection of this would have been a reasonably major undertaking for her.

We had long discussions about whether or not surgery would make a significant difference to her pain management emphasising that it was unlikely to improve her neurological function and might well lead to worsening of it. Obviously Kirsty was very keen to consider any option that might improve her pain management, but after long discussion we decided that it would not be in her best interest to undertake surgery. The other concern that we both had was that although there was one large lesion it could have been any of the others that was causing her pain. However with multiple Neurofibroma's affecting most of the nerve roots of the lumbar spine she might have embarked on a series of operations which might well have led to gradual worsening neurological function.

From my perspective, the most difficult aspect of my involvement in Kirsty's care was the fact that I was unable to do anything to significantly help her, but I am also very relieved that I have done nothing that has led to her being harmed. I no longer see Kirsty regular in clinic, but I am able to see her at any time if there are any problems that should arise.

Yours sincerely
Dictated but not signed.
John Thorne
Consultant Neurosurgeon

What other people have to say

Julie Hesmondhalgh, who plays Haley Cropper in Coronation St'

Kirsty first got in touch with me when I'd not long been in Coronation Street: a lovely letter, beautifully decorated with stickers, and containing the kind offer of being Roy and Hayley's onscreen foster child! She must have been eight at the time and I remember vividly the accompanying photograph of a gorgeous little girl with the longest, blondest hair and the bluest eyes and wearing a very posh frock! It was the start of a long and lovely friendship. I had never heard of NF until I met Kirsty, and ten years on, I'm still astonished at all that Kirsty has managed to achieve in her life, and at the seemingly unstoppable force within her -spirit, I suppose- that keeps her going and keeps her cheerful in the face of countless hospital appointments, sometimes unbearable pain and the uncertainty of what NF might bring next. She has raised hundreds of thousands of pounds for When You Wish upon a Star and is a wonderful ambassador for them, last year raising enough money to fund the entire trip to Lapland. She's a fantastic networker- an irresistible blagger,

Kirsty Ashton

borrower and cadger of stuff to auction or raffle for her now legendary balls, and is unfailingly generous: barely a week goes by without an unmistakeable sticker-adorned envelope popping through my letterbox stuffed with newspaper cuttings, breezy letters about tumour removals and day trips to Blackpool and the obligatory present for my kids.

It's impossible not to be infected by her lust for life and to be inspired by her refusal to let NF prevent her from achieving her many goals and dreams-whether they are to sing, dance and act, to swim with dolphins, to attend charity balls and Award ceremonies or to write this book.

Kirsty and her wonderful, supportive and loving family-Julie, John and Chris-have taught me so much about how to live.

Julie Hesmondhalgh

Kirsty's Story

Paediatric Dietician, Wythenshawe Hospital:

Cathy Head:

I have known Kirsty for almost 4 years. She was referred to me after losing a lot of weight following surgery. I had to try to build her up with lots of lovely supplements. Delicious weren't they, Kirsty?!

Ever since that time, I have seen Kirsty and mum regularly. I always look forward to her visits as she's full of surprises and relates interesting stories of her latest adventures. In spite of set backs, constant pain and concerns, she always greets you with a smile.

Her tireless charity work and genuine care for others in spite of her own ongoing medical problems, is an inspiration for us all.

Thank you for your friendship, Kirsty!

Cathy Head

Kirsty Ashton

Play Specialist on Starlight Ward Wythenshawe Hospital:

Pam Barnes:

My name is Pam Barnes and I work as a play specialist on the children's Starlight Ward at Wythenshawe Hospital.

I have known Kirsty since she was a tiny baby and have watched her grow up to be the beautiful young woman she is today.

Although Kirsty has a serious condition, is in constant pain and has had lots and lots of hospital admissions she remains extremely positive and Kirsty always has a ready smile for everyone and the most infectious giggle. She is enthusiastic in all she does- be it her college work, her drama, her social life, even her numerous visits to the hospital.

Added to this Kirsty cares so much about others around her – especially sick children who are going through similar experiences to her own and has worked tirelessly for "When You Wish upon a Star" charity raising thousands and thousands of pounds.

Kirsty also has a wicked sense of humour and her out-patient visits always end up with bouts of laughter in between her artistic creations at the art table. Needless to say we all look forward to Kirsty's appointments.

Of course all of this would not be possible if Kirsty didn't have the support and 100% backing of her loving family.

Cheers Kirsty! Look forward to your next fund raising events.

Pam Barnes

Kirsty's Story

CHARLES AUSTEIN VOCATIONAL SERVICE AWARD

Rotary Club Member, Linda Mullins wrote:

The Charles Austin is named after our late, long serving and much respected, honourable member.

Our club consider that the recipient of this award has qualities demanding dignity and respect, is pleasant and helpful in all conditions, has thought for others and is someone who does more that is reasonably expected of them. A none Rotarian who must live or work in the local area.

We feel we have found such a candidate in Kirsty Ashton, Kirsty suffers from Neurofibromatosis and Scoliosis, she has to wear knee, leg/foot braces and often wears a Boston body brace, she attends hospital many times a month and has had numerous operations, but despite all this she works tirelessly to raise money to send sick children to Lapland through the When you wish upon a star charity, so far Kirsty's efforts have raised £68,000.

Kirsty's interest in this charity started many years ago when she had her own wish granted with a trip to Lapland, where she met a young girl who like herself had a wonderful time on the trip, but unfortunately passed away shortly afterwards, and Kirsty said' If it hadn't been for the Charity this girl wouldn't have had her last wish granted, this inspired Kirsty to send as many children to Lapland that she could.

Kirsty lives with her parents, Julie and John and has a wonderful brother Chris, all who have supported Kirsty with her illness and her fundraising. I read a notice once that said' Families that have been given a child with a serious illness have been specially chosen by God, as the people best for the job', in the Ashton family, God chose well.

Kirsty runs her own website for anyone with the same illnesses and one quote I have picked out of this sums up who Kirsty is, "I am here as a support for you, to be a friend, someone you can sound off to when your feeling down. Anyone can tell you it won't hurt tomorrow, but I'm here to listen when it hurts today".

Kirsty Ashton

We believe that in honouring Kirsty we are saying thank you from all the people she helps every day, either through her web site or her fund raising.

Kirsty is an inspiration to me and I am sure an inspiration to all who know her, I feel honoured to have met her and wish her all the luck in the world in her fund raising and more importantly in beating her illness.

Linda Mullins

Kirsty's Story

One of my Ambulance drivers

I have known "K" a good number of years. I've seen her grow as I have driven her to her appointments. I work for the ambulance service and it is by chance we have the same surname.

I did write a short story based around "K's" life, as it unfolded before each day I arrived at her home and took her along with her mum to hospital.

We have a chat and a laugh, "K" has texted me over some thing she needed to know, and I did my best to help.

She travels to many hospitals and I have, had the chance to drive her. She manages to attend college and is always thinking of other people. She never complains about her own problems. With mum by her side she is a tower of strength and they joke that they are sisters.

"K" does a lot of work for her charity, again thinking of others and not herself. She has had numerous operations, to stem the tide of her tumours and always puts on a brave face. I call it body armour, the splints she has to wear and she uses crutches, but this does not deter her. For long distances she uses a buggy. It's strange to see such a young lady on a buggy but it keeps her independent and mobile.

She must be in lots of pain but she always has a smile on her face. She asks about everyone in the service and many have helped her.

Many articles have been written about her and T.V. programmes built around her, but she is still "K", a young lady with a major medical problem, which she doesn't allow to depress her. Always bright and cheerful, always with a bright smile and always willing to give a kind word. That's our "K".

Mr. Michael R Ashton

Kirsty Ashton

Mrs Ball, a lady who contacted me after reading my web site wrote the following Verse for me:

My Friend Kirsty

I looked on the "Post Pal" website and scanned through the girls and the boys I sent out some cards and some letters and a few little Christmas toys.

I didn't expect an answer and so it was such a surprise

When a letter arrived from Kirsty and I read it with tears in my eye's.

In spite of the N.F. she suffers, no way does it make this girl glum, she's out raising money for others and not sitting home on her …..bottom!!!

She sends lots of children to Lapland to see Santa Claus and his elves,

What excitement to look at the reindeer and see all the toys on the shelves.

It's hard work to raise all this money and continue her studies at school.

Her hospital visits are many and (she says all the drivers are "cool")

Forties Nights, raffles and auctions, badges and fundraising stalls,

Some of the people from "Corrie" attend Kirsty's Parties and Balls.

Her picture in lights up in Blackpool now Kirsty's become quite a star,

She deserves every accolade going, her fame is now spreading afar.

If ever you're feeling hard-done –by, read her story and then you will find

That you're counting your blessings by number and leaving your troubles behind.

By Mrs Marlene Ball

Kirsty's Story

WISHING ON A STAR

Wishing on a star

Rarely takes you very far

Dreams stay dreams

As thoughts and schemes

Just fade away

In the reality of each new day

But God decrees

When a star is born

It will not manifest

Till the seed sown

In wind and rain

Have gently grown

Through toil and pain

Emerging into troubled light

Like sunshine in the darkest night

With will so strong

And heart so brave

"There are children

Hurtling to an early grave"

Eyes open wide

Unaware of time

Kirsty Ashton

Don't think, don't walk

That would be a crime

Not time to dream

We are at the races

Can't you see

Those smiling faces

Every day brings something new

I know a star who makes dreams come true

**This poem was written for me
By Mr. Antony Sheldon**

Some fun times

(My life's not always revolved round hospital)

I started writing what life is like with Neurofibromatosis and Scoliosis when I was 9 years old (1999). I started having problems with my NF just before my ninth birthday and I had to start attending hospital more frequently; more so in the last four years, as My visits to the hospital have been weekly sometimes as many as four times in a week. This is due to many new internal tumours being found, which has caused new problems for me.

I don't let my hospital visits interfere with my everyday life and just take it in my stride, plus I enjoy chatting to my ambulance drivers who pick me up each week.

So let me tell you some of the fun things that have happened to me since I have been writing my story.

August 2003:
We are just back from having a wonderful holiday in Florida. I had a great holiday, but the baggies handler's at the airport broke my wheelchair. A lady called "Nancy" who worked at Sandford Airport in Florida was really helpful. We spent two days of our holiday trying to get my wheelchair mended.

We stayed in a lovely villa with its own pool, in Kissimmee. We visited

Sea World, which was beyond anything you could ever imagine in a theme park. We watched a show with a killer whale called "Shamu". Both mum and I sat in what they called the wet zone and we did get well and truly wet when Shamu swam past and splashed the audience. We went on to watch a sea lion show and a dolphin show, I really love dolphins.

Disneyworld's Magic Kingdom was indeed magic, I met Mickey Mouse, Goofy, Minnie Mouse, Donald Duck and many more Disney characters.

EPCOT, which stands for Experimental Prototype Community of Tomorrow, was the second park that we visited. They have a firework and laser show that brings the park to a close each night. They had a special place taped off for wheelchair users round the lake so we could see the firework show. It's not often you go to a theme park and come out educated but with Epcot you will as well as having lot's of fun. You'll come out with a refreshing approach to life and an appreciation of what the world is all about.

I was meant to swim with the Dolphins while I was in Florida but I was not very well and in a lot of pain so I could not manage to do it. I am really hoping I get the chance to swim with them again some day. They are lovely animals and so clever.

Remember when I made that wish when I put the heart in my teddy at the teddy factory? Well, that was my wish to swim with dolphins.

There are literally a million and one things to do in Florida.

19th September 2003:
Today was one of the best days in my life. Why? Well, I thought I was going on one my trips to the hospital this morning and that mum wanted to pop a competition entry off at Granada Studios. On the way Mum sneakily asked me if I wanted to go in with her to bring her luck with the competition (mum knew I would say "Yes").

The day began when we got out of the car and Dad said he was just going to park up while he waited for us. When we walked into the building a lady walked up to mum and shook hands and then turned to me and said, "You must be Kirsty, I am Sian Lewis from the Woman's Own Magazine, Pleased to meet you". I still did not know what was going on, I kept asking mum what was going on but she would not tell me. Then, in walked a camera crew who introduced them selves. A lady said, "I am Caroline Doherty and we are from GMTV," I was told that I was going to spend the day on the Coronation St' set with Julie Hesmondhalgh (Haley) and that my brother Chris had written this lovely letter to the Woman's Own Magazine to nominate me for the Child of Courage award (I have told you before, he is a fantastic brother). I had a marvellous day with Julie Hesmondhalgh, Sian Lewis (from Woman's Own) and the rest of the crew. It was raining but that did not spoil my day. I pulled a pint in the Rovers Return, (great fun), walked down the street, met some of the cast members, saw Roy's café, Haley's and Roy's house, the corner shop and lots more. It was truly a fantastic day. I also met Kieran (Keith Duffy) and he gave me a kiss. What a cool guy.

My story appeared in the Woman's Own Magazine (3rd November 2003) covering my day on Coronation St'.

I did not win the child of courage award, but I got down to the final 20 and I was asked if would go down to London on the 7th December 2003 to do an interview with Lorraine Kelly on GMTV Lorraine Kelly wanted to talk to me about my condition and the charity that I raise money for (When You Wish Upon a Star). This is a fantastic charity, which grants wishes for very poorly children.

GMP Young Citizen of the Year for Trafford:
Miss Lloyd, my head teacher nominated me for the title of "Young Citizen of the Year for Trafford" run by the Greater Manchester Police, for how well I cope with my illness and for the charity work I do.

I had to attend a big award ceremony where I was named the Young Citizen of the year for Trafford, which was also featured on BBC TV News. The evening was very eventful and I met lots of other students who had done remarkable things for their communities.

My first job as the Trafford young citizen was to attend the Trafford Family Police carol service where I was asked to say a few words about the charity When You Wish upon a Star.

1st DECEMBER 2003:
I was feeling a little nervous about doing the speech, but as soon as I started to talk, I felt more relaxed. At the end of my speech there was a collection for my chosen charity and I am really pleased to say the collection made over £236. 00. The evening was very enjoyable.

Kirsty Ashton

£1000, 00 TARGET REACHED:
Yes, I am pleased to I have reached my £1000, 00 target for "When You Wish Upon A Star". I managed to raise £1225, 39p, which helped send a group of 100 poorly children to Lapland to see the real Farther Christmas. I had held lots of small events to try and raise the money, but it's not always easy getting money out of people.

16th October 2004: Charity Ball:
Mum and I were asked to attend a charity Ball for "When You Wish upon a Star". So I started writing to companies to ask if they had any auction item for the event and I received a good response.

What a brilliant night, I had the shock of my life, My mum told me she was getting a taxi to the Ball and when 7pm came my brother shouted to me that the taxi had arrived. Well, this was some big taxi for outside my gate was a Limousine. It was fantastic. Katie who kindly donated a limousine ride as one of the prizes also gave me a surprise ride in her limousine, Katie was just wonderful and it really made my night. The items I managed to get to auction for the evening managed to raise over £4,000 which was really good and which meant I had managed to raise over £5,000 for this wonderful charity in just over a year. I am really pleased about that.

March 2005:
I spent the next three months in the children's hospital, but even though some of that time was spent in the High Dependency Unit and I was really not very well it was not all bad. I made many new friends and mum and I would have fun with the nurses talking about ghosts. The hospital I was in was built many, many years ago and was known for being haunted. The wards are long with about ten beds in them. Taps would turn on when no one was near them, then turn off again and one night one of the nurses sat on my bed telling mum and me about one of the parents whose child was on the ward about six months earlier. She said the parent had gone to the parents' room to make a cuppa and sat talking to another parent who was already in the room. After exchanging stories about each other's child the parent said that she had better get back to her child and with that the other parent did the same, but instead of walking through the door she walked through the wall. When the parent got back to the ward she was in a state of shock and could not speak. The nurses had to get a doctor down to see

Kirsty's Story

her. The nurse promised me the story was true and that she was not having me on.

A few days later, I asked mum if we could play a trick on the night staff, nothing too cruel, but they did keep trying to scare me. I asked mum to bring me two toy cars from the play room, which I kept by my bed so the nurses could not see them. My bed was two beds down from the nurses' station and mum was sleeping next to my bed on a reclining chair she would pull the curtains round my bed when it was getting late. On this particular night, I woke Mum about 4a.m. We could hear the nurses talking about ghosts, so I asked mum to get one of the cars, mum put her hand under the curtain and whized one of the cars up the ward towards the nurses' station. Well, you should have heard the screams from the nurses' station (good job it was only me and two other children on the ward). Mum jumped back on the chair and we both pretended to be asleep. Then we heard one of the nurses say "Go and see if Kirsty is awake". They popped their head into my bay and whispered "Kirsty, Kirsty was that. You?" but I pretended to be a sleep. The next morning, the nurses told me what had happened and asked me if I had anything to do with it, to which I said "No" and asked them to think about it. I pointed out that if I had been responsible, they would have seen me or heard me making a noise. They said "You're right, we would, but it was really scary and we thought you and your mum had been playing tricks on us". We never did tell them it was us until after I had been discharged.

While I was in hospital some very special guests paid a visit to our ward to help try cheer the children up. The Clown Doctors as they were known did not know a lot about medicine but they certainly know how to raise a smile from a child feeling not so well. The Clowns were funny and had some of the younger children playing with balloons.

The Clown Doctors provide laughter and therapeutic play to sick children and young people in hospital. They introduce themselves as Doctors but they are clumsy, forget things and do everything wrong. It's great to watch the younger children telling the clown doctors that they are doing things wrong. The clown doctors certainly brightened up our ward.

Kirsty Ashton

Spending three months in hospital felt like a life time but all the doctors and nurses were really kind and often sat on my bed for a chat.

10th June 2005: Home from hospital at last
I went to The Gentlemen's Night out Charity Committee Annual Presentation, which was being held at the Hilton Metropole Hotel, Birmingham. Some other children and I were asked to go along with the Wish Team to pick up a cheque, which the committee has kindly donated to When You Wish Upon a Star. We all had a brilliant day with lots of surprises. We played a game of stand up bingo and when it got down to the last 20 to 30 people we were all asked to go to the front of the room. This guy went across looking at the tickets and told about five of the adults to go back and sit down as he had already called one of their numbers. By the end of it the ten children from When You Wish upon a Star were the only ones left standing at the front of the room and to our surprise we were asked what our wish was. You can guess what mine was (swim with dolphins in Florida). One of the children wanted a laptop, one wanted a bike, one little girl wanted to spend Halloween in Disney land Paris and some wished for the same as me. I could not believe when this guy handed us each an envelope that said our wishes had been granted. None of our parents knew this was going to happen and a large box of tissues had to be passed round the audience.

It was a long day and I was very tired with only getting out of hospital the day before after three long months but I would not have missed this for the world.

17th June 2005:
Blackpool. The Wish team asked me if I would take part in a promotional video for them, which was being filmed in Blackpool, I had to attend hospital in the morning but I said that I would attend after my appointment. We filmed at Sea World, Blackpool Zoo, having a meal, and playing on the beach. We all had a brilliant time and the girls from the Wish team could not do enough for us. They really are a great bunch of people and you never know when you are flying away on your holidays or at a function. You may have seen the DVD we made.

Kirsty's Story

30th September 2005:
I was in the Manchester Evening News today. My brother, Christopher put me forward for the Pride of Manchester Award. I think I find out in December how well I did. If I am lucky enough to win I will win £3000, for my charity and a trophy naming me the Pride of Manchester.

The Manchester Evening
The Manchester Evening News have been fantastic in helping me with my fund raising for When You Wish Upon A Star, I asked if they would kindly put a letter on their letter page for me so that I could sell pin badges for my charity. This they did gladly and I had a fantastic response from the Evening News readers, I had lots and lots of letters and donations and sold about 350 pin badges. A big thanks goes to the Editor Paul Horrocks at the MEN for allowing my letter to be printed.

Matthew Brown's Ball, 22nd October 2005:
My friend Matthew has won a scholarship to the prestigious Guilford Drama Academy. He had to go through gruelling auditions to gain this all important place, which is a three year course. This is a dream come true for Matthew. Matthew suffers from CF (cystic fibrosis) and has worked really hard to gain his place. Friends and family held a dinner dance at the SAS Hotel, Manchester Airport to help raise money for Matthew's fees and we all had a great time. The cast from Coronation St' also came along to support the event. Mum won a TV DVD Combie in the raffle and mum gave it me for my bedroom. Love you mum.

11th November 2005:
Today I had to take the second part of my Math's GCSE paper. No more exams until the 24th November 2005 when I will have my Science paper.

3rd December 2005:
Some good friends of ours (Alan, Lesley and Stacey) helped me put together a 1940's event to help raise money for When You Wish upon a Star. We had a great night and managed to raise £1,168.00. Everyone came in 1940's dress or uniform (I wore a uniform too). I would also like to say a big thank you to Alan, Lesley, Stacey, Chris, The Royal Mail and all the companies that got involved with this event, You are all stars.

Kirsty Ashton

5th December 2005:
Today I found out that I was in the final eight to be named the Pride of Manchester, The overall winner will receive £3000, 00 for charity, which is fantastic. It now goes to a public vote and whoever gets the most readers' votes will win.

12th December 2005: Lapland
I went to Lapland with my brother to see the real Santa in Rovanie, Finland. We had to be at the airport for 5.00am. The flight was nearly three hours long but the time passed very quickly as we had breakfast on the plane and lots of fun with the celebrities who joined us on the day. When we arrived, we were transferred to the Enchanted Forest where giant bonfires burnt. We rode on skidoos, snowmobiles, had a Husky ride and met Rudolph. The Finnish people were lovely and very friendly, later we all sat in a circle in the forest and submitted to an Aretic Circle initiation ceremony. This means being flicked round the face with a reindeer tail and drinking hot chocolate, great fun. Finland only has a couple of hour's day light at this time of year and it was already going dusk when we landed. After lunch each child met Santa. This was really emotional as you watched each child going up to receive a gift from Santa. We later visited Santa's Village and Santa's Post Office, where his small helpers stamp all the children's letters from all over the world and despite me not being very well and having to see the doctor we had a great time.

The trip was organised by the When You Wish upon a Star team and over 90 children and a parent were invited. Many television stars came along too. When I got home my legs and fingers were really swollen. My mum elevated my legs up to try and get the swelling down.

25th December 2005: Christmas Day
What a fabulous time I have had, I received lots of lovely gifts from my family and friends and from Post pal. Post pal is a wonderful organisation and I have many new friends since I became a member. Post Pal helps to bring a smile to the face of a poorly child by sending letter, cards and gifts.

I also had a lovely surprise gift later in the day when mum asked me to open this large box for her.... What a surprise when I saw this electric Bass Guitar with everything to go with it, I really could not believe

Kirsty's Story

my eyes. Mum and Dad told me that this was a gift from a wonderful lady in the States by the name of Kristen Parker who wanted to buy me something that I had always wanted, well, she certainly did that. Kristen set up a website in memory of her beautiful daughter, Ashley. Please read about this remarkable young lady by visiting My Favorites' websites link.

12th January 2006: Pride of Manchester results:
Today, the name of the Pride of Manchester winner was enounced. It was based on a public vote.

The afternoon started by everyone meeting at the M.E.N where we all got to know one another a little better. Drinks and food were laid on for everyone to enjoy. After dinner we all went into the M.E.N boardroom where Neville Richardson of the Britannnia Building Society gave a sort speech about their involvement with the Pride of Manchester after, which Maria McGeoghan, deputy editor of the M.E.N gave a sort speech about each contestant before announcing the three winners in reverse order.

I could not believe it when my name was called as the winner; I was shaking and very much in shock. Everyone in that room was a winner and they had all done something remarkable. It was great having the opportunity to meet so many lovely people. I was really pleased to have won so that I could give the £3000, 00 prize over to the When You Wish upon a Star team, who do a remarkable job at putting a smile back on a sick child's face. I would like to thank everyone who voted for me both by post and by e-mail and a very BIG thank you goes to Paul Horrocks editor of the M.E.N, Maria McGeoghan, deputy editor of the M.E.N, everyone who was involved at the M.E.N and Neville Richardson of the Britannnia Building Society. Thank you for giving me a day to remember.

Kirsty Ashton

Receiving my Pride of Manchester Award from Mr. Neville Richardson

14th January 2006:
I had a surprise visit from my good friends Julie and Martha today. It was great seeing them both and Martha was just so much fun, I love to watch her play and giggle.

8h February 2006:
I called in to see the Wish Team so that I could present them with the £3000,00 cheque I won when I was voted Pride of Manchester, plus I had other cheque's for them from the 1940's event, The Royal Mail and donations that I had received.

Ruth, Sue and Sam presented me with a big bunch of flowers and tickets to watch Holiday on Ice which was such a lovely surprise.

Kirsty's Story

Ruth and Me

Sam, Me and Ruth

Kirsty Ashton

11th March 2006:
I held another 1940'S event and managed to raise £793,30p, which turned out to be another successful evening.

16th June 2006:
Today was my school Prom and I had a brilliant time. The afternoon started by me having my hair and makeup done by Gillian (Gillian does the makeup for the Corrie' stars) who is my new friend. She is really cool and we had a great afternoon together. I decided I wanted to be different from the norm' and go to my Prom in an army jeep so our friend Lee took me in his jeep, which is from the 1940's. Everyone was waving as we went by.

1st July 2006: Florida
We are off to Florida after having my wish granted to swim with dolphins. My doctor would not sign the papers last year for me to go as he said I was not well enough to travel on such a long plane journey.

After a very pleasant flight, we arrived in Florida. I was introduced to our pilot, Mark Guest, when we arrived at Orland Airport.

In flight

Kirsty's Story

Walt Disney World is made up of four distinct parks. Animal Kingdom, by far the largest.

Mum said she was just too old for rides that moved her stomach so decided to limit herself to attractions where her feet would remain on the floor.

This usually involved putting 3D glasses on in front of a big screen, then sitting in a seat having water sprayed in our face, heat blown at us and our chair back prodded and jerked.

The magic of Disney was made all the more magical by the Fast track pass, allowing you to book for later on that day instead of queuing, but having said that I was in my wheelchair and all the Disney staff went out of the way to help me.

Epcot is the most adult of the four parks and we had visited Epcot before but dad Chris wanted to go again, so mum and I headed over to Seaworld, which is part-theme park, part-aquarium. Here you can feed the dolphins and ride another suicidal roller-coaster. Seaworld is known for its killer-whale show, but we preferred the dolphin show. Dad dropped us both off and said he would call us when he was going to pick us both up.

Discovery Cove

Discovery Cove is built to look like a tropical island retreat with thatched huts, crystal-clear water and appropriately exotic insect noises (presumably recorded). The genius here is that they never allow too many people in.

I got into the water. To actually touch the dolphin and interact with the dolphin is an experience I will never forget for the rest of my life and I feel very privileged to have been able to do it.

Our dolphin was called Roxy. Very cute and smiley (aren't they all?). She was three years old – a teenager in dolphin terms.

The day is very well structured. You are assigned a time when you will swim with the dolphins on your arrival, so you get the opportunity to choose what you would most like to do for the rest of the day.

Kirsty Ashton

We spent the morning swimming with the stingrays and relaxing on the beach. We were placed in a small group of eight (we did not know the other people). We got to interact with the dolphins and play games, so I felt as though I was getting to know their personalities.

Swimming with the dolphins in Florida was an ultimate dream of mine and it came true after the When You Wish upon a Star team granted my wish.

The experience was amazing and the rest of my family enjoyed it too! This was a life changing experience that my family and I will never forget. To swim alongside these magical creatures and to receive a kiss from Roxy (our dolphin) was better than all the medicine.

We were told that the dolphins were free to swim away from us anytime they wanted to and weren't forced to do anything they didn't want to. Each of us got to kiss Roxy and our photo were taken doing so. We also got to rub the dolphin down. We were asked to hold our hand out, palm up and the dolphin swam right up to us, I sent the dolphin out to the middle of the water, and also got splashed by the dolphin as she swam past waving her fin! We then swam out to the middle of the lagoon, I went with my brother and Mum and Dad went next. Then each of us in turn held onto the dolphin while she swam back to the shore, which was a great experience. I also got to hug Roxy, feed her fish, and tickle her belly while she lay on her back. Sadly our 30 minutes in the water were soon up and we all waved goodbye to Roxy, who then lay on her side and waved back, splashing us all one last time. We all really, really loved every minute.

One day I would really love to do this all over again. It was so amazing and something that I will never forget.

Kirsty's Story

My brother Chris kissing Roxy our Dolphin

Me kissing Roxy

Kirsty Ashton

Me swimming with our Dolphin, Roxy

While I was on holiday I was often asked what the scars were on my back as I have two great long scars from where I had my spinal surgery. One goes from the top of my back down to the bottom of my back and the other from the top of my back coming round under my arm to my tummy.

I decided to make the story interesting and tell them that I was attacked by a shark and that this great 15 foot shark spotted me in the sea and decided to make a snack out of me, but I fought back., kicking and punching until it let go. The look on their faces was a picture and my shark attack story was much more interesting than saying I had spinal surgery.

G.C.S.E Results:
I received my results this week; my family says I did really well and are really proud of me. I took 15 G.C.S.E's and managed to gain 9 at A-C grade and my other 6 were still a pass but below a C. I am enrolling on a Performing Arts course at college, which will take me three years to complete. So you never know I may make my dream and become an actor on Coronation St" one day.

Kirsty's Story

1st September 2006:
I have been busy trying to get raffle and auction items for my next big fund raising event in November. Keith and Pat Oldfield who own the Printon in Cheadle have helped organise a Charity Ball for me with all money raised on the evening going to my £65,000 target to send 100 sick and terminally ill children to Lapland. I have always wanted to do a really big event like a "Ball".

My VIP Trip to Asda with Coleen Mcloughlin
I was nominated to open the Asda Store in Altrincham by a very nice gentleman, Mr. Derek Hollows, I did not know anything about this until I received a call telling me that I had been chosen. I was told I would be treated like a V.I.P and picked up in a Limo' and that Coleen and I would open the Asda store. Well, when I arrived at the Asda store there were so many people outside and TV cameras that I really did feel like a V.I.P. Everyone was so nice. After opening the Asda Store with Coleen, we both went shopping in the store and Coleen gave me lots of shopping tips. She was really cool and very friendly. I was interviewed for the TV News and later we went for a hot drink where Coleen and I chatted about my fund raising. My interview was on the TV News. I came away with lots of lovely clothes and items for my bedroom worth over £250.00.

Coleen Mcloughlin and I

Kirsty Ashton

Just before we cut the tape

October 2006:
I had to go to London for a few days, as I won the Well Child award for best brave child age 16 years and over and I was in the Best magazine the week beginning 28th November 2006. I was presented with my award by Peter Schmeichel, the greatest Goalkeeper in the history of Manchester United. I also met Dick and Dom.

I have also been busy getting ready for my Charity Ball on the 18th November 2006. It's been really hard work and I could not have made this event possible without the help of my friends, Keith and Pat Oldfield who have been brilliant and very supportive after they read my story in the Manchester Evening News. I hope to raise £10, 000.00 on the night. Julie Hesmondhalgh (Haley from Corrie'), Ian Kershaw actor/writer, Colin Bell (Manchester City Legend), Tony Martin (The Crooner) and Mr. Bernard Manning will all be attending my event.

Kirsty's Story

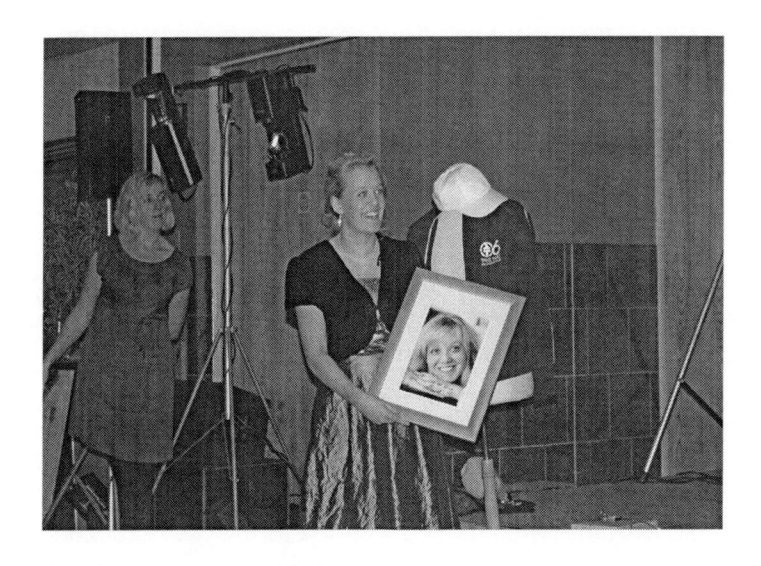

Me holding a signed picture of myself, which went for auction and raised £4,100.00

Pat, Ruth, Keith and Me handing over a cheque to Ruth for over £24.801.63p

Kirsty Ashton

22nd November 2006:
We managed to raise a staggering £24,801.63p, and although I was extremely tired for a few days after, I am really pleased with the amount we managed to raise.

Julie and Kersh worked really hard on the auction, Keith, Pat, Alex and the team from the Print On shop worked really hard to make my night a success too. I could never have done this without their help. My signed picture went at auction for £2,100.00 and I was asked to do a second one, which went for £2000, 00 bringing in £4.100.00 towards my target. I was amazed at the outcome. I got more for a signed picture of me than I did for a Jacket signed by Jason Orange from "Take That".

8th December 2006:
I was invited to London to meet Ben Shephard by Chloe and spent the morning watching him present GMTV and Entertainment Today. Mum and I had a brilliant time and Ben was just as nice as I expected him to be. I even got a hug and kiss from him. I also met some other celebrities, Jason Donavan, Andy Abraham, Michael Underwood and lots of other GMTV presenters.

14th December 2006:
Today I handed over a cheque for £24,801,63p to Ruth from "When You Wish upon a Star" with the help of Keith and Pat from the Copy Shop. Stuart Hall presented me with the Hall's Hero Award, which was a big surprise. This was on Channel M on Monday 18th December 2006.

2nd March 2007:
I am going to have a documentary made about me, which will be called The Day in The Life of Kay. Filming starts next week and will be done over two days.

I am really looking forward to doing the documentary. They are going to film me at college, hospital, at home and with my mates.

6th March 2007:
Filming went really good today. One of my mates came round and we did some filming of Dan and I at the park. We then went on to college where I was filmed doing my acting. Later in the day I had an appointment at the hospital to see my NF doctor, "Dr Sue Huson",

Kirsty's Story

which was filmed and Dr Huson also said a few words about how my NF affects me, which was really interesting and Dr Huson said she enjoyed taking part in the documentary. The film crew said they would be at my house for 8.30am tomorrow to continue with the filming.

7th March 2007:
The film crew arrived just after 9am and chatted over a cup of tea about what they wanted to film today, I had two hospital appointments. One was physio' in the hydro' pool and the other to see Cathy, my dietitian to have my weight checked.

Before mum and I were picked up by my ambulance driver they wanted to have a chat to me in my bedroom about how I felt about all my hospital appointments and what I felt about my NF and scoliosis.

Next I was filmed taking my yucky medicine. The door-bell rang and it was Phil (my ambulance driver). The film crew had already been given permission to travel in the ambulance with mum and me and they continued to film me on the way to the hospital in the ambulance.

On arrival at the hospital and while I was waiting to see Cathy, they wanted to interview my mum. They filmed in the door way of the entrance to the hospital, which was a bit mad as people kept coming in and out. When they came to do the filming with Cathy, I was waiting in the waiting room and Cathy had to walk in as she would normally do but they had to keep getting Cathy to re do it as some small children kept running in front of the camera. The interview with Cathy went really well. The crew left us to have a private chat with Cathy before we headed off to the Hydro' pool to my physio'. My poor physio' looked scared to death when see saw the camera's. The crew filmed me doing my physio', I tried not to get the camera wet.

Filming finished:
After the crew had gone home on the Wednesday, we were all really tired, I was going to go to bed but as I was not feeling so well mum asked me to stay down so that she could keep an eye on me. I am so glad I did because about an hour later we heard this funny sound coming from upstairs, which sounded like air in the pipes. When dad and I went up, the boiler in my room had burst letting out boiling hot water all over my bed, down the wall, on to the carpet. Chris (my brother) managed to

get the water shut off and got this guy he knew to come out and have a look at it. He said that I was not only lucky that I was not in the room at the time but the boiler had been giving out toxic fumes, which could have killed me in my sleep.

My bedroom was gutted. We had to get a new boiler. Mum had the new boiler moved into the loft for safety reasons. I was so upset as my teddies got ruined. The story of my boiler made the Sunday paper (The Sunday Post).

The documentary I did was on sky, the community channel on the 21st May 2007 and was repeated everyday for many weeks. You can still watch the documentary by visiting my web page and clicking on the NF link.

26th March 2007:
After the hospital on Friday I went to see the filming of "Britain's Got Talent". It was really good, I got to see Ant and Dec, Simon Cowell, Piers Morgan and Amanda Holden. The new concept for this show, required each of the three judges to light an X' if they wanted the act to get off stage. If the act managed to stay and do all their act they got to go to the next stage. It was great fun to watch.

5th April 2007:
Where do I begin to tell you what a brilliant Birthday I had?

My morning started with me waking up at my grans' (my mums, mum) due to the accident with my boiler, I still cannot sleep at home. When I got home and after opening all my lovely gifts from family, my friends at the hospital and post pal and blowing my candles out, which took some doing, Mum mentioned that we were going out. She said that I needed to be ready for 5.30pm as we were going for a meal before going to watch a show at the Lowry called the ECLIPS, a circus musical, which Julie, Kersh and Martha had treated mum and me to for my Birthday.

When 5.30pm came Dad asked me to get in the car so that we could get going and as we went round the corner on our estate Dad stopped the car and asked me to get out, I could not believe my eyes when I saw Paddy (one of the best Limo' drivers you could wish to meet, the other being Paul). As a Birthday treat, Paddy and Paul had arranged to pick me up in their brand new Limo' Chrysler 300 C (Hemi/Bentley) limousine... what a car...what a drive... it was fantastic.

Mum and I arrived at The Deansgate (where we were having our meal) and we were met outside by Colin (Paul's brother) who escorted us to our seats.

It was all really yummy and we were both bursting after. Colin is a brilliant cook.

Paddy then took us on to the Lowry to watch Eclipse; we had the best seats in the house and the show was amazing. Eclipse is a journey of the seasons through the elements of earth, wind, fire and water. It had an international cast of talented artistes, telling a dramatic fantasy tale ballet, mime, song, dance, aerialists, juggling, rhythmic gymnasts and acrobats. I loved the playful jugglers. You've seen nothing until you've seen Eclipse, the UK's first and only circus musical. After the show Paddy brought us back home in the limo'. The next day Paddy and Paul called round with a big bunch of flowers and a box of chocolates.

28th April 2007:
I held a 1940's charity night, which went really well and I managed to raise over £1,400.00. Everyone got into the spirit of the night and came dressed in 1940's style clothing and we had 1940's music playing. A brilliant night was had by all at the same time as raising money for some very brave children.

I went to a party at Julie's and while I was there I met Rob (Liam out of Corrie') and Rupert (Jamie out of Corrie'). I had a great time and did not get home till after 2am.

30th June 2007:
Mum and I have been invited to have lunch with Prince Harry and Prince William today at Wembely.

Mum and I had a great time meeting Prince William and Prince Harry. I spoke with Prince William. He asked me what I thought about the Spice Girls getting back together and what bands did I liked best. He then spoke about WellChild and wanted to know how I became involved with them, Prince William was taken aback when I told him how much money I had raised and wanted to know what I had done to raise so much money. After chatting with Prince William, we went for a meal. After the meal we had a photo call with Prince William and Prince Harry, I was asked to sit next to Prince William, then we went into the Royal Box at Wembley to watch some of the concert that was being put on in memory of Diana. I was asked to do an interview for the BBC News, Sky TV and Radio. The day was brilliant and everyone was so kind.

23rd July 2007:
It's my mum's Birthday and for part of my mums Birthday prezzi' I took Mum to have some pictures done with me. We had a make over done and I think we look good together.

Mum and Me

24th July 2007:
I went for my theory driving test today and I am pleased to say I passed getting only one question wrong I am now going to start my driving lessons so be **WARNED** I will be on the road lol.......

Susanna who lives in the U.S.A sent me a lovely package I had been feeling a little unwell when I received this box full of teddies, which really made my day.

14th August 2007:
Both mum and I went to watch the "The Antony Cotton" (Anthony plays in Corrie') show being filmed and it was really enjoyable. The show went out on TV last night and both mum and I were featured on the show in the audience. On her way to the shops, Mum was asked by someone who had seen the show if she had been in audience. Fame at last.

8th October 2007: 10th Anniversary Black & White wish Ball
Mum, Dad and I went to the When You Wish upon a Star Black & White Ball on Saturday night and we had a brilliant time.

It was held at the Palace Hotel in Manchester. We were entertained by Eton Road (what great guys), the cast from Corrie' who were brilliant, Kym Ryder (Michelle) sang a few numbers as did Michael Starke (Jerry) most famous for his role as Brookside's 'Sinbad', Could he sing? We were blown over by his singing voice,

Katherine Kelly (Becky) sang a few numbers. So many more of the Corrie' cast sang too and were really good.

My good friend, Paul Crone was there too and I had a go at him for not having the guts to ride on the Big One at Blackpool while eating and drinking with me. My very good friends Julie Hesmondhalgh and Kersh (Ian) were there too. The night was just fantastic and lots of money was raised so that the poorly children on the When You Wish Upon a Star book can continue to have their wishes granted.

Kirsty Ashton

Ian Kershaw, Me and Julie Hesmondhalgh

I am off to watch a play at the Oldham Coliseum Theatre on Friday called "Union Street", which was written by my good friend Ian Kershaw. Union Street is a bitter sweet comedy about young love, broken dreams and the changing face of our town.

10th November 2007:
I am going to a charity party tonight at Lightbowne Sports & Social Club, for When You Wish upon a Star, This is made possible by the hard work of Sue, Connie, Joan, Chris and Trish. They have arranged the fund raising night with curry and hot pot supper I have been asked to give a speech about When You Wish upon a Star and about the wish that I had granted last years.

4th January 2008:
Well, I had a really nice Christmas and Santa was very good to me again this year, I received lots of lovely gifts and cards from post pal.

Kirsty's Story

I am now getting busy for my big Valentine Ball in February, I could not have managed to have this Ball without the help of my good friends Keith, Pat and Alex, who do all the hard work and all my printing for me, I just get in the way I write to companies and to the stars to get them to come along or donate auction and raffle items.

9th February 2008:
I have had a busy few weeks. Channel M contacted me and asked if they could come and interview me for WellChild and talk about my condition and Charity Ball that I am having. I was on Channel M on Monday 4th February.

I was also asked to do a live TV interview for Channel 5 on Thursday 7th February. Both mum and I went down to London to do the interview for Channel 5 News.

14th February 2008:
Getting very excited now my Charity Ball is on Saturday, Keith, Pat and Alex have helped me so much to make this Ball a success I can't begin to find the words to thank them all.

I have been asked to do a live TV interview on Monday morning, 18th February 2008 for channel M, where I will talk about how my Ball went. I will be on the breakfast show.

The Manchester Evening News will be covering the story too and coming along on the night to take pictures.

18th February 2008:
My charity Ball went really well, I had over 200 guest including Julie (Haley from Corrie'), Ian Kershaw (actor/writer), the boys from Eton Road, Rowetta from X- factor, The Mersey Beetles and Vince Miller. Guests travelled from as far away as Holland, Scotland and London. Some of my doctors and nurses also attended. Lots of money was raised.

14th March 2008:
I am really pleased to say my Valentine Ball raised a whopping £23, 000, 00 and I presented the cheque to Carole from the Wish Team on Thursday, 13th March along with "Eton Road" (David, Marcus, Danny and James) and Keith and Pat Oldfield.

Kirsty Ashton

5th April 2008:
My 18th Birthday, I had a great Birthday even though I did not pass my driving test. Lets face it, I can always take it again so I was not going to let it ruin my big day.

I had so many birthday cards from all over the Globe (54 cards in total). People who had read my story on Post Pal sent me gifts too. The team from Wish upon a Star sent me a lovely bottle of champagne, a teddy and a box of chocolates. My friends from the Copy Shop Pat, Keith and Alex sent me a large bunch of red roses, Julie called round with gifts and my friend Emily sent me a teddy, Susanna my friend in the USA sent me a box of teddies and lots of other gifts, I also received lots of money from family members, as well as gifts from Mrs. Ball and Becky and gifts from some people who I don't even know. Everyone has been so kind.

11th April 2008:
The postman knocked on our door this morning and handed me a large box that contained three balloons wishing me a happy Birthday and a bag of mini eggs. When I read the tag it was from Kate Dee, Kate is one of my friends from Post Pal.

Manchester Hero Award:
Someone has nominated me for the Manchester Hero Award, in association with Barclays and M.E.N, I don't know who it was, but all I have been told is that a few people have put my name forward for the award. I was in the Manchester Evening News on Wednesday, I was in hospital due to have an operation and one of the doctors came up to me and said "We have a celebrity on the ward" and I asked him who it was? and he said "You". He had just read about me in the paper. I really thought we had a celebrity on the ward too. I was also on the Channel M, TV, News over the award. I was a little embarrassed because I did not know why I had been nominated really.

Thank you to all my doctors, nurses, family and friends for getting me through some of my difficult times.

17th April 2008:

Kirsty's Story

I received a call to tell me I am in the final five to be named a Huggable Bear Hero and if I am one of the two winners from the UK I have to go to Washington DC in July to receive my award.

4th June 2008:
Today I found out when I opened the M.E.N that I am one of the 25 winners of the Manchester Hero award and will be going to a presentation night next Thursday 12th May, I have won £1000, 00. I am going to use the money to try and help get this book published.

12th June 2008:
This evening, Mum and I went to the Manchester Hero Awards, which was sponsored by Barclays and M.E.N as it prepares to open it's flagship branch on Market St. The awards honours some exceptional people from across Greater Manchester. The 25 winners came from all walks of life, from have a go heroes to another young boy who raise's money for charity. I felt honoured to be part of the celebration. Kym Ryder presented the awards. We each received £1000, 00 and a framed certificate.

I would like to say "Thank you" to the Manchester Evening News, Barclays Bank and to all the people who nominated me for the award.

Kirsty Ashton

13th June 2008:
They say Friday the 13th is unlucky for some. Well, this was not an unlucky day for me.

Mum said we were going to the Trafford Centre to get my grans' teddy from the Build a Bear work shop I was busy looking round when the next thing I knew Helen (the manager) came up to me holding a beautiful bunch of flowers and a teddy and told me that I had won the huggable bear hero award for the UK and would be flying out to Washington DC in July to receive my award, which means money for my charity and a scholarship to University, I was in total shock and could not believe it. Channel M filmed it all and later interviewed me, which was on TV this evening.

8th July 2008:
Mum and I are off to Washington, DC this morning for the Huggable Bear Hero Awards so it was up at 5.30am for us both as we have to be at the airport for 7am. Dad arrived home early from his night shift so that he could take us.

I had been told that one of the Build a Bear Associates was going along too and that his name was Chris. He was traveling from the same airport so I knew he would be on the same flight, I had been told what he looked like and when I arrived at the airport both mum and I saw this young man standing with an older man. We looked at each other and we both said "Chris". Being cheeky, I went up to him in my wheelchair and asked if he was called Chris to which he replied "Yes" looking at me in amazement, I then asked "Are you from Build a Bear" and he said "Yes". So I introduced myself and my mum and we stayed together for the rest of the journey.

The flight over to New York was really good and the food was nice too. But we had a four hour delay with our connecting plane. So we were all very tired after just having had a seven hour plane journey. When we eventually boarded the plane in NY it was really small and I got out of my wheelchair to board the plane, Mum was told to leave the wheelchair at the side and that they would fold it up and make sure it was put on the plane. Unfortunately they had problems trying to fold it and a member of the crew had to get mum to do it. As mum got up she bumped her head on the over head baggage compartment (shows

Kirsty's Story

you how small the plane was), I know shouldn't have but I went in to the fit of giggles along with half the plane, Poor mum. Mum folded the chair and we were on our way finally getting to our hotel at 10.30pm Washington DC time, so it was like 3.30am for us and we had been up almost 24 hours.

We were picked up in a limo' and taken to the hotel where we were met in reception by a very nice lady from Build a Bear, she asked us to order a meal and drink and that she would see us in the morning. When I went up to our room there waiting for me on the table was this basket of goodies from Maxine Clark. We were really tired and managed to get a great nights sleep, the beds were so comfy.

9th July 2008:
We were up early as we had to be at breakfast for 7am due to the busy day that we had ahead of us. After mum and I had finished breakfast, I just had time to head back to our room and get showered before it was time for my photo shoot. I was told I would feel like a star for the day, which I did. I had my hair and make-up done before heading over to the stylist who had a selection of clothing and trainers for me to try on. I chose this really cool multi coloured jacket, a green top, pink trainers and a pair of sweat jeans (the jeans cost over £100.00). A few weeks earlier I had picked and dressed two teddies, one that represented me (I put a blonde wig on it, holding an i-pod) and one other teddy just for fun. I was photographed holding one of the teddies. While I was busy doing my photo shoot, mum was being interviewed in this other room about my charity work and about me (I hope she said some nice things). After the photo shoot I was told that I could keep all the clothes that I had chosen apart from the jeans as they had only borrowed the jeans for the shoot and they had to give them back. They were really comfy too. After the photo-shoot, it was time for me to be interviewed. By now it was getting on for 11.30am and almost time for lunch. We all had to meet in the Capital Room C in the hotel as we were having a Lunch N' Learn as a Group. We had the opportunity to meet and learn from some of the beary special partners with whom Build-A-Bear Workshop works.

I also got to meet all the other 2008 Huggable Heroes, who were:

Kirsty Ashton

Anna – Colorado, Austin – Arizona, Aymeric - France, Christina – New York, Dallas – Washington, Emma – Nova Scotia, Jack – Oakville, Michala – Kentucky, Rocco - New Jersey, Jasmine – California, there were also two Associate Huggable Heroes who were: Christopher, Warrington and Laura, Wisconsin. There was one other winner Malka – London but Malka was unable to attend the awards. Every one of the above names have done something good for their community, which is why they have been honored in this way.

After lunch I attended a Leadership Symposium with some of the other Huggable Heroes. We all participated in a special leadership symposium with a lady called Kathy Cramer. We got into two groups and worked together as a group. The Leadership Symposium lasted about two hours.

By now it was 4.30pm and mum and I were free to relax for two hours. We went for a little walk around Washington DC but not knowing the area we did not want to go to far and both being on crutches we could not go far anyway. We did attempt to find the White House but went the wrong way.

We all had to meet in the hotel reception for 6.15pm as we were going to the Hard Rock Café for tea. By now all the previous five year Huggable Hero Winners had arrived to mark the fifth year of the awards. Lots of hugs were being passed around, which was nice to see.

The Hard Rock Café had stained-glass windows and honours the rock-and-roll greatest stars. It was really busy and we waited a while for our food to arrive. We got back to the hotel about 10.30pm and all decided to meet up in the hotel swimming pool where we stayed until midnight. Mum and Debbie sat in the hot tub by the pool.

10th July 2008:
Breakfast was not as early this morning so we got a little to lie in until 7am and down for breakfast at 8.00 am. At breakfast we were joined by Millicent Williams, Executive Director of Service DC.

After breakfast all Huggable Heroes from this year and the previous four years departed to do some community service activity. We all had a turn at painting a beary special mural at Lackie Elementary. For

Kirsty's Story

lunch we all sat in a big group having a picnic lunch. Leaving our mark in Washington DC felt really good.

Getting back to our hotel for about 4.00pm, gave us two hours to relax and get changed before heading off for the Huggable Bear Hero Awards. The awards took place at the Top of the Hill with Chief Executive Maxine Clark and Olympic Gold Medal Gymnast, Dominique Dawes, who served as the evening's MC and Michelle Rhee, Chancellor of the DC Public School system who was one of the keynote speakers. The room was done out beautifully and each table had two teddies on it. The meal was chicken and tasted really yummy. After everyone had finished their meal each one of this year's Huggable Heroes was called up to receive his or her award from Maxine Clark. I was first up and while I was going up for the award Dominique Dawes spoke about what I had done to receive the award as she did for each of the heroes. The evening was very interesting and memorable. We got back to the hotel about 11.00pm and after having a chat in the hotel reception we decided we would all meet back down in the hotel pool for one last splash about. We went back to our rooms at about 12.30am.

11th July 2008:
We were up early for breakfast, I had a quick chat with some of the new friends that I had made and then went to get some gifts to take back home while mum went to do the packing. I was given four new teddies, a set of clothes, a book (which Maxine had written) and lots of other nice things so mum had a bit of a job fitting everything in the case. We were picked up at 12pm to take us back to the airport in the biggest Limo' I have ever seen. There were fifteen of us in including our entire luggage and my wheelchair, so that will give you an idea of how big it was. Chris and his dad, Nigel were on the same flight as us so we stayed together. We got back to Manchester just after 7am on Saturday morning. The last few days have been amazing; everyone involved went out of their way to make it memorable. Both mum and I met and made friends with some pretty amazing people from all over the Globe and we now intend to keeping in contact with them. I can't wait to see the Build a Bear calendar when it comes out later this year.

29th July 2008:
This evening my Mum and I were invited to the Didsbury and District Rotary Club meeting where I was presented with the Charles Austin

Kirsty Ashton

Volcational Service Award. The award is named after the late, long serving and much respected, honourable member of the Rotary Club.

I was nominated for this award by members of the Rotary Club, which made even more special. The evening started with us having a three course meal followed by coffee. Linda made a speech about why I was being given the award (which I have included in my book) and presented me with a Certificate, £200, 00 for my charity, a portable DVD player and a bunch of flowers. Linda then passed over to Phil, Phil said a few words and then presented me with another Certificate and a cheque for £100, 00 for me to take my family out for a meal. The evening was very interesting and both my mum and I were made very welcome.

15th August 2008:
My picture (head and shoulder shot) is to be transformed into a 1960's pop art style image. The design called local Heads will use photographic portraits and put them up in lights in a 60s pop-art style, which will then go on display as part of a quarter mile long archway of faces which will take pride of place along Blackpool's promenade throughout the Illuminations season for the next three years. I was one of six chosen by Granada Reports.

My Picture in Lights at Blackpool

Kirsty's Story

19th September 2008:
I have just returned from my two week trip to Disney World Florida with my Mum and Dad, there is so much that people take for granted when taking a holiday, which can be a huge hassle for us. For example, before I was even allowed out of the country I have to be insured (not easy to get with all the problems that I have) and documents need to be signed by my Doctor so that I can take my medication out of the country, then I have to make sure I have got leg room on the plane because I can't bend my legs with the leg braces on. But everything went smoothly and I had the time of my life. Disney world was fantastic and we had so much fun. With the incredibly infectious songs that play again and again throughout the Disney parks. We got to meet Mickey Mouse, Pluto, Goofy, Mini Mouse and lots of other Disney characters. We also met up with some good friends of ours, Andy, Melissa, Amie and Louie, it was great to see them as we had not seen them for a while. We also met with Melissa's mum who was over visiting the family. Andy, introduced us to some of his friends (Ryan and Mike) who I will tell you more about as I tell you about my holidays.

After having tea and cakes with Andy, Melissa and the children, Andy introduced us to Mike who owns a Segway business in Celebration and after giving mum, dad and I a course on how to ride a Segway Mike kindly took us all out on a one and half hour ride round Celebration and on to a nature trail. I was surprised at how well my mum did on it, dad on the other hand needed the most training. But like all men he kept making excuses..lol. While on our holiday we visited Epcot. Ryan (Andy's friend) from Dream Tours took us round the Epcot Park and got us on all the rides with his fast pass.

Epcot is one of my favourite Disney parks. It allows you to travel round the world to China, Japan, Germany, Great Britain, and other countries without leaving the USA or the need for a passport.

We went on lots of rides and my mum even went on Test track (a fast ride for my mum). I will not be going on Mission Space again... I don't like getting motion sickness, dad felt really ill when he came off this ride and so did Robert a friend of Ryan's who came on the ride with us, mum had already decided she was not going to ride it and sat and had a coffee with Ryan while they waited for us to finish the ride.

Kirsty Ashton

Magic Kingdom has gone from my second favourite park to my favourite park (just in front of Epcot).

Magic Kingdom is situated on its own Island, so to get there; you will have to travel by monorail, or the Mississippi steam boat. We used the monorail. There were characters all over the park in designated spots, and the queues were well managed. I managed to get the autographs of some of the characters, and then had photos taken. As you stand at one end of Main Street, and look towards the centre of the park, Cinderella's Castle is the first thing to strike you. We all went on the Splash Mountain ride and as I wanted to sit at the front with my mum we both got really wet. It is a log flume style ride which starts inside through a character village with cartoon type alligator, and then heads outside for the ride. Prepare to get very wet. I went on Thunder Mountain Railroad, which is like a runaway mine train. Mum and Dad would not come on this ride.

Then we went on the Haunted Mansion ride. You sit in a car, and it takes you round the mansion, and out into the garden. At one point, you come across a mirror, and there is a ghost sat in the car with you, certainly good for freaking out young children.

We went on lots of different rides and had a brilliant day. Towards the evening we lined up to watch the Parade, which was great fun and lovely to watch the colourful fibrotic floats, the many Disney characters and beautiful music that they had playing. We then watched the fireworks, which looked over the colour changing Castle.

Typhoon Lagoon, which is a water Park and an amazing park, we had an awesome time here! The rides were crazy, mum enjoyed the Lazy River, it was a perfect way to relax. We also decided to go to Blizzard Beach to ride the water slides and play in the pool. Our first stop was to find a place to "camp" – a term that means to have a place to return to when we want to rest.

Our first ride was the Double Tube slide. It was great. The walk up the mountain to get to the entrance of the slides was a bit too much for my mum and me. Mum and I were looking for the oxygen relief at the first set of stairs! However, the slide was well worth it! Next it was onto the Toboggan Racer Slide with my dad. This was incredible! You lie down on your belly and use the more traditional water slide mats – except these have handles, which you need to hold on to and you literally fly down the slopes. Eight lanes of racers launch each time down straight lanes that drop at different intervals. We were exhausted. Each night before we went to bed we said we were getting up early the next day, but each morning, we did not get up until at least 9 a.m. We went on a ghost hunting tour of Kissimmee and managed to get some really cool pictures. I really did have a great holiday. But I missed my brother as Chris was working and not able to come with us.

27th October 2008:
I was asked by the Build a Bear work shop if I would go and help with children in Need fund raising event they were having at the Trafford Centre on Wednesday. The morning went really well and the young children had a great time playing games and dancing about. I had my face painted to look like Pudsey Bear.

27th November 2008:
I have been nominated for the Manchester Community Award and have just found out that I am in the finals and will be attending a presentation evening on the 10th December when I will find out if I am one of the winners.

On the 11th December I am in a performance at college, which I will be marked on for my grades, I should of been in a performance on the 10th December too, but my tutor "Pete" kindly allowed me to have the evening off so that I can attend the awards evening. "Thank You Pete".

10th December 2008:
I attended the Manchester Community Awards this evening with my mum, Brad and good friend, Lesley. I was in the final three to be named "The Young Citizen of the Year". The finalists were honoured at a glitzy Town Hall ceremony, hosted by the Lord Mayor of Manchester and Gordon Burns off BBC North West Tonight. The event was made possible by generous sponsorship support from a number of Manchester businesses which provide services to the communities of Manchester and have a commitment to improving the quality of life for residents. A special champagne reception for all the guests attending the glamorous ceremony was hosted by Xerox, in the Lord Mayor's Parlour. I was

shocked when my name was called out as the winner. I received a large glass trophy with my name engraved on it and £300. My award was sponsored by Northwards Housing. Martin Joyce, Managing Director of Enterprise Manchester, who sponsored the Pride of Manchester Award said: "Enterprise Manchester are very proud to award Gloria Barnwell the Pride of Manchester in recognition of her invaluable contribution to Manchester's communities. He also referred to the unprecedented decision they made to award an extra "runner up" in the category, adding: "We are also very pleased to make a special commendation to Kirsty Ashton in the Pride of Manchester category, for her remarkable achievements in the face of adversity." For this I received a further £250.00, a framed certificate and a £500.00 donation to my charity. I would like to say a big thank you to everyone involved in the awards the night was most enjoyable and well done to the entire winner's:

Anne Tucker from Rusholme won the Contribution to the Environment Award, Gina Hall won the award for Creativity in the Community, Karen Harris and Gwen Davies, who run the Manchester Stingers Women's Football Club, Connie Strongitharm from Longsight won the Lifetime Achievement award, Gordon Binns The Good Neighbour Award and Gloria Barnwell, who won two of the award categories: Citizen of the Year and Contribution to the Community. I would like to say well done to all the runners up too. It was great being in room full of wonderful people. The entertainer for the night was "The Crooner", if you have been following my blog you will know that Tony, The Crooner attended my first charity Ball, he is such a great guy with a fantastic voice. It was lovely to see him again.

11th December 2008:
Tonight was my college performance, why is it you always get a cold when you have perform in front of people. Lol..... Never mind, it went well and everyone enjoyed the evening.

17th December 2008:
I was given the biggest surprise of my life, I went to college like any normal day, dressed like a scaly, I had this nagging cold, so did not really feel like lessons. Peter (my tutor) asked me to lead the lesson, I was doing my work when Calvin Valentine (Ricky Whittle) entered the room with a camera crew and said "I'm looking for Kirsty Ashton", I was like eer, eer," Hi"! He said "do you know why I'm here"? I said "no", he

Kirsty's Story

said "well come over here and give me a cuddle". He said I had done so much for other poorly children, that they had decided to do something for me and that he was going to take me to Liverpool to look round the Hollyoaks set and that I would meet the cast, I was buzzing. I went in Ricky's car to Liverpool (some cool car that he's got I can tell you). Ricky showed me round the Hollyoaks set, which was being filmed the whole time, he then said I hear you like Andy who plays Rhys, I was like erm, "no comment, I think you are all fit" lol... Ricky introduced me to Newt (Nico Mirallergo), then Rhys spoke to me and I was all googly eyed. We had some pictures taken before going for dinner. After dinner I went and watched Ricky do his scene. Ricky then surprised me and told me that I have been given a part in the pub scene with Rhys and Gilly, I was like WOW, I was given my script and asked to learn my lines ect while I was in make-up. I had to flirt with Rhys (not a difficult for me to flirt), Rhys rubbed it in because he knew I liked him, when we went off set the cameraman asked for picture of us both, Rhys was going in for the kiss and then he fell and the camera man went we might have one of it looking like you're going to kiss lol. Then there like, keep in contact ect' and hopefully see you back here one day. I spoke to the director, he said he was impressed and that I was easy to work with ect' so you never know I could be a regular one day. After my scene we ended it off with a bit of me waiting in the pub and then the lovely sexy Calvin came in the pub in his uniform, it was an image to die for, I was like OMG, OMG I am going to faint, he looked sooo fit, but I love them all, they are all brilliant. Hopefully we will stay mates and stuff and I'll see them on set again someday. I have heard from Ricky (Calvin), Andrew (Rhys), Anthony (Gilly) and Sonny (Josh) since I have been back. I really did have the best day of my life and I would like to say a big thank you to everyone involved in making my wish come true.

To act in Hollyoaks was on my wish list in my book. I can now tick that one off. But I would love to do more acting on Hollyoaks, I loved it so much. I met some of the nicest people, I cannot remember all your names so thank you to everyone, Paul Young, jay Morris, Ricky, Andrew, Nicole, the camera crew, and all on Hollyoaks for giving me a brilliant day.

Kirsty Ashton

Outside my college just after Ricky Whittle sprung the surprise on me

6th January 2009:
I am still buzzing from my trip to Liverpool and don't think I'll believe I have been on the Hollyoak's set until I have watched it on TV. I am going on Noel's HQ to talk about my day on Hollyoaks (can't wait to meet Noel), mum loves him too and watches him every night on Deal or No Deal, we both applied to go on it some months back, but not heard anything yet lol..

18th January 2009:
I was on Noel's HQ on Saturday night the 17th January 2009. I had a fantastic time on Noels HQ. When we arrived at our Hotel we had a bit of bother with the room as it only had one bed in it, but they soon changed our room for us and they apologized for what had happened. After getting a good night sleep, I wanted to visit the National Portrait Gallery as I am doing my "A" level's in photography and came away with some good idea's to help me when taking pictures. When I got back to our hotel I had a little rest before going for a quick shower and change of clothes. Mum got a call to say our car would be with us in 5 min's. When we arrived at the studio's our car was met by Paul Young and Jay Morris, people had already started to queue to come in and watch the show and the show was not for another two hours. I felt like a star as

Kirsty's Story

both Paul and Jay kissed me on the cheek and took me inside. You can imagine my surprise when I was shown my own dressing room with my name above the door. The room was huge and had a TV, video, fridge, toilet, shower, fridge (which was filled to the top with drinks), the room was Huge. Noel was in the next room to mine, I so much wanted to knock and ask him who the Banker was lol...Paul, Jay, Nicole, Ross and lots of other people kept coming in to make sure we were all ok and asking if we wanted anything. I was then taken to make-up; I had to look glam before going on TV. We were then seated in the studio ready for the show to start, I began to feel nervous and my hands were shaking. Was first on so I was then taken back stage ready for Noel to call me on. Noel called me on to stage and gave me a hug and told everyone what I had done and short film of my day on Hollyoaks was shown. Then to my surprise Ricky walked on stage, when he saw me he ran up to me and gave me a big hug. Ricky also presented me with a signed copy of my script from all the boys on Hollyoaks and a signed picture of me flirting with Rhys, which now takes pride of place on the living room wall.

After the Noel's HQ had finished everyone who had been on the show including the stares and crew all went back stage for drinks and food. Neil Fox came chatting to me and congratulated me on raising so much money. I got lots more hugs of Ricky (I am now in love). I could not believe it when Noel said Ricky was here too as you will have seen by my face. Ricky is such a nice guy and gives nice hugs too. I chatted with Keith Chegwin and Noel, mum asked Noel who the Bankers was and he said "sorry, can't tell you, not even for you" lol. We had a great night and everyone was really nice. I had something money just cannot buy, a part on Hollyoaks and I would like to thank Noel Edmonds and Ricky Whittle and everyone involved in making my dream come true. And Ricky Whittle, "I love you". Lol I have had lots of feedback from people saying how I have now inspired them to do something for charity, if everyone did a little something the world would be a much better place.

20th February 2009:
Yesterday mum and I went to London where I did a fashion shoot for the Daily Mirror, my hair and make-up was done by CB (Claire) and I was styled by Oriella Paganuzzi, I had a great time. My pictures were taken by Emma Cattell who made me feel so relaxed when taken my

photos. All three were really nice and made both my mum and me very welcoming to the studio. They even made us butties and kept us in drinks.

27th February 2009:
What a busy day I have had today. My day started with me doing a radio interview with BBC 1 Radio Manchester, I was on 7.30am breakfast show with Eamonn O'Neal and Dianne Oxberry. I spoke about the book I have written, my appearance on Hollyoaks and about the fundraising that I have done for When You Wish upon a Star. Off air we had a little private chat. Then my brother took me to London as I had an audition at 1.30pm and another audition at 2.45pm. it was a good job my brother was off work and able to be my taxi for the day, I would not of been able to do both without his help. "Thank You, Chris" you are a great brother.

17th March 2009:

Today I was in the Daily Mirror, I was given a full centre page spread. The Mirror had arranged for me to do a photo shoot to help me with my modeling and TV work. I was contacted by a number of magazines who also want to cover my story after reading about me in the Mirror.

27th April 2009:
Now for some good news! On Friday I went to Edinburgh as I was nominated by Linda and Phil from the Didsbury Rotary Club, for a Rotary Young Citizen Award and was one of the five winners to receive the award. It was really nice to get away for a few days. It was a long drive but we stopped at the service station for food and drinks, we didn't arrive in Edinburgh until after 4pm, On the evening we arrived I went to see McFly in concert with one of the other winners (Leanne), Leanne's parents and my mum. I had to be at the Corn Exchange for 6.45pm.

When I arrived at the venue I was given the surprising news that I was to meet the boys from McFly. Both Leanne, her parents, my mum and me were taken round the back of the venue and introduced to the boys, they were great and after giving us a big hug they chatted about why we had been given the award, they were shocked when they were told how much I had raised. We then had some picture taken before

Kirsty's Story

going to watch the boys on stage with all the other girls screaming in excitement. I was surprised when McFly mentioned me on stage and everyone clapped and cheered me when McFly had finished talking about me.

On the Saturday morning we had to be at the Corn Exchange for 10.15am so that I could have a quick interview with Konnie Huq who was presenting the awards live on the BBC News 24. Konnie was a presenter on Blue Peter for ten years before leaving the show last year. We arrived at the Corn Exchange just in time thanks to Linda's good driving and my good navigation system around Edinburgh, which was a nightmare to drive round due to all the road works they have going on at the moment. I met with the other winners before being sat on stage ready for the awards to go out live on the BBC News at 11.30am. There were over 2000, Rotary members from all over the world in the audience, I was a bit nervous as I had just been sick before going on stage and was worried in case it started again while I was on stage. I was the last winner to go up and Konnie asked me a few questions and showed a short film about me as Eve had been to film me in hospital the week before and had also filmed the girls from Wish Upon a Star and one my doctors, Mr. Neil Oxborrow. I managed to make the audience laugh a couple of times with my answers, which is always a good thing. I received a lovely glass trophy and a certificate and I am told I have also got £500.00 to come to me for my charity, which will go towards my target. After the ceremony we had lunch and some more pictures taken on stage. Lots of people kept coming up to me and congratulating me on my award and some gave me money towards my next target, all in all I was given £80.00 for my charity. While mum and I was out I saw the Top Gear presenters, Richard Hammond, Jeremy Clarkson and James May, mum asked if I could have my picture taken with Richard but this woman said "No" but I still took some of Richard and Clarkson. Linda than rang my mum to say she was on her way to pick us up so that we could all go for tea before heading back to the Corn Exchange to watch a concert. It was a Scottish Variety Performance. I had arranged to meet Leanne (one of the other winners) at the concert and we all sat together. I must say we really enjoyed it. The show finished about 11pm, I was shattered by the time we got back to the guest house. I kept ringing my dad to find out how my 1940's event back home was going as I had left dad in charge of the raffle for me. Dad rang me when

Kirsty Ashton

I got back to the guest house to say the raffle had raised £390.00 with money still to come in. Thanks for doing the raffle for me dad. Before going home on the Sunday we went to the morning Rotary Conference, which was really interesting. The RT Hon Michael Portillo did a speech and told some really good jokes. Then it was time for the long journey back home. A massive thank you to Linda for all the driving she did and Phil and Linda for looking after us so well over the weekend and of course for nominating me in the first place.

23rd May 2009:
Last Saturday, mum, dad, and me went to the Chester football club to watch the Hollyoaks lads playing football against other soap stars. The Hollyoaks team included my man Ricky Whittle (Calvin), Nick Pickard (Tony), James Lomas (Warren) and lots of other cast from Hollyoaks. They played against some of the cast from Coronation Street, Emmerdale, Shameless, Casualty and the Bill. They were playing to raise money for two charities. We all had a great day even if it did rain. All the guys came round and chatted with us after the game and I got a big hug off Ricky when he saw me.

June 2009:
I am trying to arrange to do a Spookathon, which would mean me staying in a haunted house over night. I have got some of my ambulance drivers and some other medical people who are involved in my care willing to do it with me so if I can pull it off we should raise lots of money.

12th July 2009:
I have been back to see Mcfly in concert in Nottingham with my friend Leanne, we both had a brilliant time, I stayed over at Leanne's for the weekend as she lives in Nottingham. Thanks to Leanne's parents for making me so welcome.

August 2009:
I am doing my spookathon in November and hope to raise lots of money for my charity,

I have passed my exams and I have been excepted into Chester University to study TV/Radio Media, mum and dad said they are very proud of me as I am the only one in the family to ever have gone to University, which

Kirsty's Story

made me feel really happy. Next week I am going to our local Rotary club, where I have been asked if I will do a speech about my condition and the charity that I raise money for, which should be interesting.

8th October 2009:
I have been over to Florida with my mum and dad, we had a great time. We met up with our good friends Andy, Melissa and children, Amie and Louie, we had not seen the children for year and it was great to see them Amie was so big and Louie was chatting away. Melissa came ghost hunting with us, which was great fun, dad got us lost and we could not find the car. Visiting one of the water parks dad went swimming with the car keys and lost them, luckily someone found them and handed them in. but when we tried to start the car it was having no go and we had to sit in a car park for over an hour until we had another car brought to us, we could not go back in the water park as it was getting ready to close so we baked in the sun for over an hour.

You will never guess what my mum did, she forgot to pack my Gabapentin tablets, which I have three times a day for the pain in my back. We tried to buy some but was told they could only be got on prescription, my brother, Chris, was going to post them out using the next day delivery service. When he inquired how much it would be the post office said it would £100.00 to send a package next day delivery, but when he told them what was in the package he was told he could not post them, he even contacted the Embassy to explain things to them but the person he spoke too was unsure if they could be posted to the USA. In the end I had to use my Ketamine, which makes me feel dizzy if I have it in the day, I normally try and only have my ketamine when I have gone to bed.

Then mum had an accident, we were attempting to play crazy golf, I had my go and so had my friend, then it was mums turn and as she picked the golf ball up her knee gave way and she fell back smacking the back of her head on a concrete path (she was seeing stars), we heard the bump and dad just came over and said "look I got an hole in one" , and I said "and your wife as just smacked the back of her head". It did look funny seeing mum lay with her legs in the air and I am sorry for laughing mum. My friend went and got an ice pack from the people who owned the golf course. Mum had a big lump on the back of her head for the rest of the holiday. We still had a great holiday and no harm done in the end.

29th November 2009:
My charity spook night was really good, it's hard to believe but lots did happen and when the channel M guy (Ben) was filming a fire extinguisher came flying off the wall but they could not show it on TV as a couple of people swore in shock, one guy got scratched on the back of his head, which must be 4ins + in length, we had some pebbles slung towards us and other people experienced some things too. Danny Morris came and supported my event and his manager "Paul" agreed to do a lone vigil in the strong room for half an hour and raised £100.00 by doing it.

2nd December 2009:
I was invited to 11 Downing St in London to meet The Chancellor of the Exchequer, Rt Hon Alistair Darling MP. I received the Diana Gold Award along with nine other young people who had all won the Diana Award over the past ten years and the gold award was to mark the tenth anniversary of the Diana awards. Over the last ten years the Diana trust has awarded 27.000 awards to young people. We had drinks and food with some other guests, including the Chancellor's wife, Maggie Darling, and Bee Gee Robin Gibb, who is an ambassador for the Diana award. I was the seventh person to go up for the award; I was given a framed certificate and a lovely glass trophy. I also gave a small speech and lots of pictures were taken for the press.

Kirsty's Story

Receiving my award

15th January 2010:
I had a great Christmas with my family and it was nice to spend some more time with my Gran (my mum's mum). Gran got herself this toy dog called "Biscuit" I love it and so does my gran, you ask it to sit and give you it's paw, it will, ask it lie down and it will, it also barks and whimpers, it really is very cute. My gran is so funny with it and keeps telling me that it is keeping her awake at night with its barking. I have also been a member of Post Pal for many years and I received lots of nice gifts from people who had read my story, one lady (Wendy) saw that I was on crutches and she bought me some really cool blue crutches for Christmas, they are so much nicer than the ones I had. We also went to the annual quiz night that our friends Keith and Pat have every year for all their friends at Christmas (Keith and Pat have helped me lot over the years by helping the organise the charity Balls that I have had. it was great to see Keith and Pat as I have not seen them for a while and Andy and Melissa had come over from the USA with the children (Andy is Keith's and Pat son), Andy always does the quiz and very good at it

he is too. Alex, is their other son and I have not seen him for a while so it really is nice to get together with everyone and one of their friends makes the nicest hotpot ever.

January 2010:
I took my mum and our friend Lesley to watch Jeremy Kyle being filmed last week, which was good fun, our friend Lesley was told to shut up by Jeremy because she was laughing, then he said she was an old woman (I don't think you are old Lesley) and next week I am going to watch the TV awards in London, which I am looking forward too.

February 2010:
NF is a life-long condition, and you must learn to live your life, and not let the disorder rule your life. The more you understand the more you will be in control, so be sure to ask questions of your medical professionals. Find someone you trust, and share your feelings, fears and frustrations. The challenges posed by having NF are hard, but they can be overcome and you are not alone. They say a problem shared is a problem halved. You can always email my mum or me and we will both do what we can to help. I hope one day we can say 'We have found a cure for NF'. "Neurofibromatosis is now history."

Although NF is a wide ranging disorder, each of us who have NF shares a common bond. NF does not necessarily bring each of us severe complications, but it does bring each of us a measure of uncertainty. No doctor can tell you how your NF will affect you, because they don't know. NF is different for everyone.

The sharing of information and support can be valuable. Each one of us has a unique life experience in living with NF which we may find beneficial to share. If you would like to share your story about life with NF, mild or complicated alike, then please sign into my guest book or email me and let's help each other today.

My story, my journey continues and I will not let NF win! I hope by having my book published it will help you fight this cruel condition too. In the meantime please don't forget if I can help you in anyway please let me know, I can't help answer any serious medical questions, but I can help you with anything that may be worrying you, or help you understand what will be happening to you. My website is not meant to

Kirsty's Story

be technical or full of medical jargon. I'm there as a support for you, to be a friend, someone you can sound-off at when you're feeling down. If you need any advice, or just want somewhere you can meet fellow sufferers then this is the place to be!

While people of any age will struggle to adjust to a life with pain it can be particularly hard for teenagers and those in their early 20s. At a time when the world should be opening up, offering exciting things, it can feel as if a door has slammed shut instead. Don't dwell on what you can't do, but concentrate on what you can, explore new interests. If I can offer support to anyone, please contact me. We are all here to help each other. That is a gift we can give each other. Thank you for reading my story.

Thank you to all my doctors, nurses, family and friends for getting me through some of my difficult times.

Take care Love Kirsty x x

Kirsty Ashton

My Goal - Fund raising

Through helping When You Wish upon a Star I have developed strength, determination and patience to achieve my goals. Fundraising is an important part of life and if I can help bring a smile to another child then I'm happy.

When You Wish Upon a Star is a small national charity whose aim is to make dreams come true for children with terminal and incurable illnesses. The work the charity does is reliant on the support of volunteers and unpaid individuals - meaning the money goes where it should - to make dreams come true for some very special children

If you have a happy, healthy child in your home you can understand what a joy it brings to see them smile.

For these brave and courageous children, many of whom undergo more harsh and painful treatments than any adult, could ever imagine, the need to bring some magic into their lives is of paramount importance, not only for them, but for their families who so bravely fight alongside them.

The sad reality is that along the way so many children have lost the battle to the terrible diseases and conditions from which they have suffered. If you could see the joy and happiness that making their special wish brings, you would understand why When You Wish upon a Star means so much to me.

Wishes are as individual as the children themselves. For a sick child, this could mean meeting a favourite pop group, swimming with dolphins in Florida, meeting a celebrity, riding in a Ferrari, Meeting Santa in Lapland the list is endless! But the joy it brings to the child and to his or hers family is unforgettable.

I know all this because I have been one of those children to have a wish granted and I know how much it helped me. Knowing I was going to swim with dolphins in Florida helped me cope with some very difficult times

I hope When You Wish upon a Star never have to turn down a child's special request due to lack of funds, as they aim to bring a sparkle into the life of the poorly child no matter how big or small the wish maybe.

My goal is to raise £145,000.00, which will be split into £65,000.00 to send 100 poorly children to Lapland to see the real Santa and £80,000.00 to send 30 poorly children and their families to Centre Parc's for a five day holiday. If you think you can help in anyway please contact me via my web site at www.kirstysstory.co.uk and please help bring a smile to some brave child today. You can also visit my just giving link, which is a safe and secure way of donating money to When You Wish upon a Star. "Thank you".

Some of the Celebrities that I have met

Bruno Langley

Sue Cleaver

Kirsty's Story

Dick and Dom

Michael Underwood

Kirsty Ashton

Anthony Cotton

Ben Sheppard

Eamonn O'Neal

Jason Donavan

Julie Hesmondhalgh

Stuart Hall

Kirsty's Story

Paul Crone

Eton Road

Stuart Flinders

Michael Starke

Kirsty's Story

Kym Ryder

Konnie Huq

Neil Fox

Keith Chegwin, Me Noel Edmonds

Kirsty's Story

Julie Hesmondhalgh

Kirsty Ashton

Ricky Whittle

Kirsty's Story

Andrew Moss

Prince William

Ricky Whittle

Kirsty's Story

Robert (Liam Conner)

Kirsty Ashton

Jamie (Rupert Hill)

Kirsty's Story

Andrew Moss

Supporters

My story was in the Manchester Evening News after I had won an award for how well I cope with my condition and for the fund raising I have done for other poorly children, which I really enjoy doing.

I wrote a letter to the MEN asking if any readers would like to buy a pin badge and if any reader had any unwanted items that I could put in a raffle to raise money. The response was fantastic.

One of the MEN readers who contacted me was Mr. Keith Oldfield who came round to my house with a digi camera worth £300.00 for me to raffle. We sat and chatted for a while and Keith mentioned that he owned a printing business (the Printon Shop, Cheadle) and offered to do all my printing for me for free. Since then Keith and my family have become great friends with the Oldfield family and with out the help of Keith and his lovely wife Pat I would not have been able to have the two charity Ball's that I have had. They really are amazing friends. "Thank You" Keith and Pat for everything you have done for me.

Mr. Derek Hollows also read about me in the MEN,

Mr. Hollows owns his own paper shop and offered to place my wishy box in his shop, which has helped to raise lots of money too.

Mr. Hollows has written his own book, which is called, As I Recall and is about the Bevin Boy's, a very interesting story. The book also honours the Bevin Boys who tragically lost their lives from 1943 to 1948 and the thousands of miners world wide who, during the course of their labours, have made the ultimate sacrifice.

Kirsty's Story

Pat, Ruth (from Wish upon a Star), Keith and I

If you would like a copy of this book please go to my web page and look under the link books for sale for more information, or you can contact me direct.

Mr. Hollows use to be an English teacher and very kindly offered to go over my book for me, putting any spelling and grammar mistakes to right for me. "Thank you" for your help. Mr. Hollows.

"Thank you" to the Editor of the Manchester Evening News, M.E.N Staff and all M.E.N readers who have very kindly sent donations to help my target for other poorly children.

Mr. E Archer, (now my adopted granddad), thank you for your continued support. Mr Archer also read about me in the M.E.N and has continued to support my efforts along with Mr. M Kelly who also read about me in the M.E.N. Mrs Betty Pickard another M.E.N reader who often sends me donations for the poorly children.

Kirsty Ashton

Mr and Mrs Singleton, thank you for the signed items that you have managed to obtain for me over the years as you know they have helped to bring in much needed funds for the poorly children. Mr and Mrs Singleton read about me in the Manchester Evening News and decided they wanted to help me.

The M.E.N readers have all been very supportive towards me and I am very grateful to you all.

"Thank you" to all at Channel M for keeping my story in the media eyes. You have been a great help.

Eton Road, Former X Factor finalists, for coming and singing at my events for free,

Alan, Lesley and Stacey Bates and my brother Chris for helping to organise the 1940's events, they always go down well and have helped to raise lots of money towards my targets for other poorly children.

Kirsty's Story

My Goals in life

I have a list of goals and a list of people I want to meet. I have just met one of my favourite bands, "Eton Road" when they came to my Charity Valentine Ball in February 2008. I have written a list of other things, which I would like to achieve, people I would like to meet and places I would like to visit. I have managed to tick a few of them off my list.

I would like to meet and sing with (not that I can sing):

- Lee Otway
- West Life
- Michael Buble
- Oliver James
-

I would like to meet:

- Darren (off Hollyoaks)
- Sean William Scott
- Ashton Kutcher
- Danny Young
- Simon Cowell (that's for my mum really)
- Richard Branson (so I can get lots of tips off him on to raise money for my charity)
-

Things I want to do:

- Have my book published
- Play a part in Holly Oaks (achieved this now)
- Be in an a TV advert
- Have a large Star Studded Charity Ball (for my charity)
- Sky Dive down a building for charity
- Stay overnight in an Haunted House for charity (achieved this now)
- Work on a proper radio station

- Work back stage on a film set
- Raise lots and lots of money
- Have my own car (achieved this now)
- Model for a Top Magazine
- Have my hair styled by a top hair stylist
- Ride in a Helicopter
- Have dinner with the cast from Holly Oaks
-

Places I want to visit (1st class):

- New York
- Sydney Australia
- California
- Hollywood
- Las Vegas
- Niagara Falls
- New Zealand
- Los Angeles

Charities

When You Wish Upon a Star:
Without this charity I wouldn't have been able to do, or get through some of the difficult times I have had. I am now an ambassador for the When You Wish Upon a Star team in Stockport

They have played a big part in my recovery in various ways. So I thank the When You Wish upon a Star team in Stockport for this. Meeting Santa and swimming with Dolphins is an unforgettable experience.

'When You Wish upon a Star provides wishes for as many brave and courageous children as possible. Each day brings requests to meet celebrities, drive a Formula One racing car, and of course every child's dream is to meet Mickey Mouse.

For the parents of a sick child, the need to make this wish come true is of the up most importance. Making their wish come true is a real boost for the sick children and their families. The children have to suffer gruelling treatments and long stays in hospital. Being able to look forward to a wonderful treat is sometimes the inspiration needed to keep the whole family going.

To keep wishes coming in for these poorly children please visit my just giving link, which is a safe and secure site. You can find the link on my web page at

www.kirstysstory.co.uk "Thank you".

When You Wish Upon a Star

www.whenyouwishuponastar.org.uk

Kirsty's Story

Post Pal:
I joined Post Pal in 2005. This is a web site for poorly children and the aim of the site is to post a smile on a sick child's face. Each child is given his or her own web page which hold further details. The page is updated monthly and contains a forwarding address for the child.

Anyone can write or post a gift to as many of the children they wish to contact to cheer them up when they are feeling poorly.

I have received cards, letters and gifts from all over the globe. I mentioned on my Post Pal page how much I love soft toys; I have received so many now and each one has made me smile. If you have a spare few minutes, please visit and write a letter to one of the poorly children and sit back and know you have helped put a smile on a poorly child's face.

www.postpals.co.uk

Neurofibromatosis (NF)
The Neurofibromatosis Association (NfA) is a medical charity dedicated to the provision of support, advice and help to those affected by the genetic disorder neurofibromatosis (Nf).

Currently there are some 25,000 children and adults affeced by the disorder in this country. Approximately half those affected inherited the disorder from a parent, but the other 50% will have developed it through new gene mutation.

At present there is no known cure, but the NfA is committed to funding research into this little known disorder.

Through the Neurofibromatosis Association's network of regional co-ordinators, the charity is able to offer help, support and advice to those affected, their families and those concerned with their care. If you can help please contact the following address giving my name (Kirsty Ashton).

Kirsty Ashton

The Neurofibromatosis Association
Quayside House
38 High Street
Kingston upon Thames
Surrey
KT1 1HL
United Kingdom

Manchester Children's Hospital
The New Children's Hospital Appeal was launched in May 2006 and is a brand new charitable appeal supporting the new state-of-the-art children's hospital currently under construction in Central Manchester.

The appeal is spearheaded by Bob the Builder and aims to raise £20 million to support projects within the new children's hospital.

The appeal will provide:

- The latest equipment for treatment and diagnosis
- Accommodation to allow families to remain together during their child's stay in hospital.
-

I have spent many months in the Children's hospital and have a lot to thank the doctors and nurse's for. If you would like to help in some way please visit the following web site for more information.

www.newchildrenshospitalappeal.org.uk/

WellChild
WellChild, the UK's children's health charity, has been working to improve children's health for more than 25 years. Today there are 15 million children in the UK. More are surviving chronic illness than ever before. Their need has never been greater.

WellChild aims to make every child as healthy as possible, support every family with a sick child, and raise awareness of children's health and healthcare.

www.wellchild.org.uk

Glossary

Anaesthetic	(Local anaesthetic) A drug used to numb a part of the body. (general anaesthetic) Used to put a patient to sleep during surgery.
Anaesthetist	A doctor who specialies in giving patients anaestheties.
Benign	Describes a non cancerous tumour or non life threatening condition.
Bone Scan	A technique to create images of bones on a computer screen or on film. A small amount of radioactive material is injected into a blood vessel and travels through the bloodstream; it collects in the bones and is detected by a scanner.
Boston Brace	A Boston Brace is a very hard jacket, and goes from the top of your chest to the bottom of your hips to support the spine.

Biopsy	To have a small sample of tissue taken to be examined.
Cannula	A small tube which is inserted into a vein in your arm or the back of your hand, to inject fluid or connected up to a drip.
CT Scan	CT stands for Computerised Tomography. A type of x-ray that uses a computer to create lots of cross sectional images.
Dermatologist	A doctor who specialise in the treatment of skin conditions.
Dietician	Person trained to provide advice on diet during illness and using diet to manage symptoms.
Foot Drop	This describes the condition when a person cannot flex their ankle upwards towards the knee (opposite of pointing your toe)

Gabapentin	Gabapentin (brand name: Neurontin®) was initially synthesized to mimic the structure of GABA for the treatment of epilepsy. Presently, gabapentin is widely used as a medication to relieve pain, especially neuropathic pain. .
Gamma Camera	A gamma camera is an imaging device, most commonly used as a medical imaging device in nuclear medicine. It produces images of the distribution of gamma ray emitting radionuclides.
Gastroparesis	Also called delayed gastric emptying, is a disorder in which the stomach takes too long to empty its contents.
Hydrotherapy	Physiotherapy carried out in warm water.
Ketamine	Is used to treat types of pain that have not been relieved by conventional painkillers.
Neurofibromatosis type 1	An hereditary condition, also called NF1

Neurofibromatosis type 2	An hereditary condition, also called NF2
Neurosurgeon	A doctor who specialises in the brain and spinal cord.
Occupational Therapist	Someone trained to help people manage their daily routine, e.g. dressing, cooking and getting around.
Paediatrician	A doctor who specialises in treating children.
Paralysis	A term used to describe the loss of the ability to move muscles, e.g. arms and legs.
PET Scan	A PET scan is a way to find cancer in the body. The patient is given radioactive glucose (sugar) through a vein. A scanner then tracks the glucose in the body.

Physiotherapist	Someone who specialises in the treatment that uses physical movement and exercise to relieve stiffness after surgery or injury.
Polycal	Polycal Powder is a Food for Special Medical Purposes
Radiographer	Someone who takes x-rays
Scoliosis	A condition which causes the spine to curve.
Spinal Cord	A column of nervous tissues in the spinal column that sends messages between the brain and the rest of your body.
Tumour	An abnormal swelling on or in the body can be called a tumour. They can be either benign or malignant.

Scandishake	Scandishake Mix is a Food for Special Medical Purposes for use ... Scandishake Mix can be used to supplement the diet of patients ...
Ultrasound Scan	A way of producing pictures of inside of the body using sound waves.
Whiplash	When muscles, ligaments and tendons in the neck have stretched and strained, often caused by a sudden jerk or jolt to the body.

Acknowledgements

I hope you have enjoyed reading my story and that it has helped give you a better understanding of how a person can be affected by Neurofibromatosis and Scoliosis.

There are so many people I have to thank, if you are not mentioned please don't think I'm not grateful to you, I am.

To all the doctors and nurses who have cared for me over the past 19 years, especially Mr. Neil Oxborrow, Dr. Smyrniou, Dr. Hill, Dr Sue Huson, Mr Thorn and Mary Brennan who is my nurse at my doctor's surgery.

Thank you too to the children's nurses at Wythenshawe Hospital and Manchester's Pendlebury Children's Hospital and thank you to Pain Team at Sheffield Children's Hospital.

To all my family and friends, especially Julie Hesmondhalgh and Ian Kershaw you have both helped me so much through some difficult times. Thank you for always being there for me and supporting me at my events. Both you and Kersh are brilliant mates.

My good friends, Keith, Pat and Alex Oldfield. You stuck by me when it really mattered and without your help I would never have achieved my goal in helping other poorly children. You understood how important it was to me to raise money so that wishes could be granted for other poorly children and I'll never forget you for that.

Thank you to my ambulance drivers who kindly take mum and me to the hospital every week. You know I love you all and to my Dietician (Cathy Head), I love our chats on a Wednesday and I'm sorry I don't eat all the food you ask me to. But I know you understand why I can't.

Thank you to my physio's who have helped me so much with our weekly workouts both in and out of the hydro' pool. Don't think I'll ever want to go over to the adult physio'. Thank you to Pam (play leader) and nurses on the paediatric clinic at Wythenshawe Hospital I don't think I'll ever grow up Pam lol...

Thank you to my Ronnie gran (mum's mum), to my gran and granddad (dad's mum and dad), I love you all.

Finally and most importantly to my mum, dad and brother (Chris). You are what keeps me going, keeps me laughing and looking forward to another day. I love you all.

"I am here as a support for you, to be a friend, someone you can sound off to when your feeling down. Anyone can tell you it won't hurt tomorrow, but I'm here to listen when it hurts today".

Lot of love

Kirsty xxx

www.kirstysstory.co.uk